ESSENTIA

TEACHING AN

SPELLING

THE ESSENTIAL SPELLING LIST,
set out on pages 41–86,
is printed separately
for classroom use.

ESSENTIALS IN
TEACHING AND TESTING
SPELLING

NEW EDITION

Fred. J. Schonell
M.A., Ph.D., D.Lit., F.B.Ps.S.

*Formerly Vice-Chancellor
of Queensland University*

Pamela Wise

*Teacher, London Borough
of Waltham Forest*

First edition 1932
Reprinted 29 times
Second edition 1985

10 9 8 7 6 5 4
00 99 98 97 96 95 94 93 92 91

Published by
MACMILLAN EDUCATION LTD
Houndmills, Basingstoke, Hampshire RG21 2XS
and London
Companies and representatives
throughout the world

Printed in Hong Kong

British Library Cataloguing in Publication Data
Schonell, Fred J.
Essentials in teaching and testing spelling.
New ed.
1. English language—Orthography and spelling
2. English language—Study and teaching
I. Title II. Wise, Pamela
428.1'07'1   B1574
ISBN 0 – 333 – 39137 – 3

CONTENTS

PREFACE

This new edition provides a structured programme for teaching spelling. All three sections of Schonell's original edition have been extensively revised.

The most important revision concerns the dictation passages which are used for assessing and developing spelling skills. Schonell's original passages had become gradually out of date, mainly because they contained references which are no longer relevant or applicable (e.g., 'the Governor General of New Zealand'). Now there is an entirely new set of dictations which are written in a lively and modern style that should appeal both to teachers and pupils.

Schonell's introduction has been left unaltered as his ideas on spelling can still provide a valuable contribution to current teaching methods. However, this edition also includes a completely new introduction which discusses the problems likely to occur in a modern school, such as teaching a mixed ability class. It also gives advice about teaching methods and suggests a variety of activities which will assist teachers to go beyond a narrow rote-learning approach to spelling.

The final revision concerns the Essential Spelling List itself. This is the core of Schonell's spelling method and therefore has been left entirely in its original form. However, we have included a list of additional words which have been grouped into appropriate graded levels. The new words are frequently used by children and tend to reflect the recent advances in technology (e.g., 'computer', 'shuttle', 'television' and 'video').

This revised edition of Schonell's work provides teachers with a carefully graded spelling list of 3 200 words, which are supplemented with 60 enjoyable dictation passages. When used together, these two sections will enable spelling to be taught in a structured and systematic manner, and the ideas and activities in the new introduction will make the lessons lively and interesting.

Pamela Wise

INTRODUCTION TO THE NEW EDITION

1 The Spelling Lists

The *Essentials in Teaching and Testing Spelling* is made up of three sections: the introduction, the spelling lists and the dictation passages. However, the spelling lists are the core of the book because they will form the foundation of all the spelling tuition. They have been designed to equip teachers with a structured and graded system for teaching spelling to children of all ages and abilities.

There are six major levels of difficulty, each of which has been sectioned off into a separate group. Group 1 contains material for the early stages by only including words with simple letter strings; e.g.,

man	get	run
can	wet	gun
ran	let	sun
met	fun	ant

It is also important to note that at this level all the words will be within a child's existing vocabulary.

After the initial stage, Groups 2, 3 and 4 provide a gradual progression through the intermediate levels until the final level of difficulty is reached in Groups 5 and 6. The last group is suitable for older or more able children since it includes words of complex letter construction; e.g.,

university	social	precious
opportunity	artificial	gracious
possibility	especially	delicious
responsibility	musician	suspicious
curiosity	triumph	suspicion
charity ability	brooch stomach	wreath

1

This arrangement of strict grading will permit the teacher to select accurately the level of difficulty which is most suitable for her pupils. Within each of the six main groups the words have been sub-divided into smaller units. These lists are usually a collection of words which share the same visual pattern; e.g.,

GROUP 2	rake	**GROUP 4**	vanish
	wake		banish
	awake		perish
			parish

Occasionally, however, the words are grouped according to common usage; e.g.,

GROUP 3	hammer	**GROUP 5**	Europe
	bench		Asia
	blade		India
	wire		Australia
			Russia

Studying words which contain the same visual pattern is an important aspect in the teaching of spelling. Modern researchers, such as Margaret Peters, emphasise that spelling skills will be most readily achieved if children have their attention drawn to frequently occurring letter patterns. It is in this way that children learn to recognise and eventually utilise the regularities in our written language. We rely heavily on the appearance of a word when attempting to spell and Schonell's lists concentrate a child's attention upon words which contain the same letter strings, even when they do not make the same sound; e.g.,

GROUP 4	stain
	contain
	captain
	Britain

Apart from considering the level of difficulty and the letter patterns, Schonell also took into account the needs of children at any given stage in their development. The word 'downstairs' appears in Group 2 whereas 'envy', which is ostensibly an easier word to spell, does not occur until Group 5. Schonell recognised that 'downstairs' would be necessary to many children, while 'envy' is more likely to be used by older children.

Schonell also carefully avoided any potential problems when he arranged the words. He ensured that any homonyms, such as 'won' and 'one', are well separated from each other as children are frequently confused if they are presented with both words at the same time. For the same reason he also kept apart any letter blends which frequently have the same sound; e.g., aw/or and ow/ou. In these instances it is always advisable for one of the words, or blends, to be fully mastered before the children are exposed to the alternative spelling. If confusion is allowed to occur it can often become so firmly established that it is hard to rectify. Quite simply children should only be taught words that *look* the same.

The word lists in this book are exactly the same as those contained in the first edition of *The Essentials in Teaching and Testing Spelling*. After considerable debate it was decided that the original lists should be left completely unaltered. The main reason for this decision was that Schonell had compiled the lists in a rigidly logical order and any attempt to make revisions would have upset the precision of his arrangements. The lists contain more than three thousand words and yet careful study showed that less than thirty of these could be reasonably replaced by modern alternatives. It would have been extremely unwise to jeopardise the overall structure in order to make such minor changes. Therefore the lists do contain a very small number of words, such as oxen (Group 2), draper (Group 4) and guinea (Group 5) which are no longer in common usage. None of these words has been used in the dictations and no great emphasis should be placed on teaching them. They will, however, provide an opportunity for enriching children's vocabulary. In order to assist the teacher here is a list of the words which have declined in usage:

GROUP 1	GROUP 2	GROUP 3	GROUP 4	GROUP 5	GROUP 6
oxen	inch	stockings	draper	bushel	wireless
(penny)	maid	inches	grate	guinea	
(cart)	(cane)		kindle	ounce	
			quart	(pasture)	
			shilling	(lantern)	

(Words in brackets indicate less decline in usage.)

Although the original lists remain unchanged this new edition of the book does include some additional words which reflect the needs of a modern child. During the last few years the major advances in technology have introduced a vast number of new words into our vocabulary. Very few children would not be completely familiar with such words as video, calculator or computer. There are also many domestic applicances which would have been unknown to a child in Schonell's time but are now considered as everyday necessities (e.g., 'fridge', 'television' and 'radio'). These and many other words, including the vocabulary for metric measurement, recent forms of transport and words related to our multi-cultural society have been organised into supplementary lists, which can be found on p. 84. They have been grouped in exactly the same way as Schonell's lists. However, there are only five main levels of difficulty since it was felt that the words were not generally suitable for the initial stages. The words have been sub-divided according to visual pattern or usage in the same way as the original lists; e.g.,

cheque	shuttle		jeans
antique	battery		anorak
mosque	lottery		sweater
plaque	cassette		trainers
metric	litre	gram	metre

By adopting the same careful structure as Schonell, these new words can now be taught in the rational and systematic way that is recommended as the most successful strategy for teaching spelling.

Given below are a small number of words that are also frequently used by children. However, because of their visual pattern there was no satisfactory way of including them in the supplementary lists. They can either be taught separately or as the need arises.

jet	torch	culture
zip	burger	commuter
jog	helmet	vegetarian
cola	guitar	
lorry	laser	

The Essential Spelling List will provide a valuable basis for any method of teaching spelling and there are a variety of ways in which it can be used. Schonell designed the lists so that a small number of related words could be taught on four consecutive days. The number of words in a daily unit varies from three to five according to the level of difficulty. On the fifth day the work can be consolidated. By the end of the week the children will have learnt between twelve and twenty words involving a variety of letter patterns. After three or four weeks the children should be given a dictation passage which includes a selection of the learned words. This activity reinforces the work and highlights any problems. This is a basic outline of the method proposed by Schonell, but there is no reason why teachers should feel obliged to adopt this system.

Rather than allocating a small amount of time each day to the spelling list some teachers may prefer to teach the words during one session a week. Any discussion and activities related to the words could take place during this time. Alternatively although all the words are introduced in the first lesson, reinforcement can continue throughout the week.

In other cases there will be no classroom activities associated with learning the lists. The children will memorise the words in their own time and be tested at a later date. This last method may have the advantage of saving lesson time but it cannot be too strongly emphasised that the greatest value of the Essential Spelling List can only be derived if the words are integrated into a combined system of reinforcement activities and dictation exercises. Suggestions for games and activities are included on p. 11.

The rate of progress and the choice of activities will be largely determined by the abilities of the children. Less able children often cannot assimilate the letter patterns unless they are thoroughly reinforced by supporting activities. Unlike the other members of the class the remedial children will also need to spend more time on each letter pattern. Instead of asking them to learn all twelve words during a week they will benefit by devoting this amount of time to just one of the patterns which is presented in a daily unit. For example, they could spend an entire week mastering '– an' from 'man', 'can', and 'ran' in Group 1. The list should be supplemented with work which includes other examples of this pattern. The following week they can begin work on the next list; i.e. 'get', 'wet', 'let'. Progress will seem to be painfully slow but the children will be developing solid foundations at a rate that is appropriate to their abilities. On p. 22 there is advice on how to deal with the problems which arise in classes that include children of widely varying abilities and levels of achievement.

The Essential Spelling List provides an organised and systematic selection of words, but it should be used with judgement and discretion. The speed of teaching and the activities that are used to reinforce the learning must always be relevant to the needs of the children. The graded levels and the precise grouping of words will assist the teacher in devising a structured scheme of work for teaching spelling at all stages of development.

2 The Dictations

It is intended that use of the dictation passages should be totally integrated with the teaching of the word lists. The two sections are directly related in levels of difficulty and vocabulary, and when combined they form the basis of a systematic learning programme.

The revised dictations retain the same structure as Schonell's original reviews. The passages are graded into six levels of difficulty which correspond directly to the main groups of words. This means that there is an equivalent set of ten dictation passages for each of the major spelling groups; i.e. in Group 3 there are ten sets of words and ten corresponding dictation passages.

Each dictation incorporates a selection of words that have appeared in three or four consecutive sets within a particular level; e.g., in Group 4 Dictation 31 uses the vocabulary from the four sets indicated as D31 on p. 62. For purposes of revision the passages also include words from the previous groups. In the earlier stages the passages only contain words that occur in the Essential Spelling List, but later dictations incorporate some vocabulary that is not included in the book. This will enable the children to practise their spelling skills when writing unknown words.

The revised passages are representative of a style that is more appropriate to a contemporary child. The subject matter has been carefully chosen to appeal to the interests of children, and each dictation is, as far as possible, a self-contained mini-story. All the usual ingredients of excitement, magic and humour have been included in stories about oil fields, spies, ghosts and super-heroes. The topics are closely related to those which children are now experiencing through television, films and books. If children are presented with familiar and interesting passages then they will associate writing as being a pleasurable activity.

Below is a dictation from Group 2. It incorporates words from many of the previous lists, but it is mainly intended to practise the four sets of words in D12. (p. 48). To assist the teacher these words have been underlined.

It was cold and damp and the road seemed to <u>shine</u> in the <u>mist</u>. The <u>driver</u> left his car and <u>stood</u> under a <u>street</u> lamp. He was <u>safe</u> at last.

The three men had chased him for a long way but he had a fast car and in the end he had lost them. He lifted the lid of his case and took out a small black book. This was what the men were after. It was very late but he had to stay awake. It was not over yet.

The dictation passages are only used every three or four weeks and some teachers may feel that their classes require more practice. Certainly in the case of slower children who are only learning a small number of words each week it is often necessary to give them short dictations which involve the learned words. There is no reason why teachers should not give extra dictation exercises to supplement the passages which have been provided.

Dictation exercises have a great many values apart from consolidating the spelling work. Among other things they will give the children the confidence to write freely on their own, and encourage them to spell words automatically and instinctively.

3 Teaching Spelling

(a) The Importance of Accurate Spelling

Writing should be a precise and satisfying means of communication, in which a child is capable of expressing his ideas accurately and coherently. The work of a poor speller is neither precise nor satisfying, for either the reader or the writer. The reader is continually distracted from the context by each misspelling that is encountered. This influences his or her judgement of the work, leaving a poor impression of the writer. But even more important is the effect that poor spelling techniques will have upon the child as a writer. He must be given the skills which will enable him to write with as much fluency and confidence as he speaks.

If a child is unable to spell he will resort to certain tactics in order to compensate for, or camouflage, his disability. One method that children employ is to discard the word they really wish to use and substitute one which they can easily spell. This results in the fact that their writing ceases to be a true reflection of their original ideas. One aspect of good writing is the application of the right word at the right time; it is not achieved by using inadequate alternatives simply because they are easier to spell.

Children are not always tempted to use simpler words; instead they will stop writing and spend time trying to work out the spelling of a

7

desired word. Their attempts may or may not be successful, but the important point is that their flow of ideas is broken by what should be an unnecessary activity. If children are given the techniques of spelling then their writing will not be disturbed by constant pauses to ponder about the letters in a word. The child's hand will quickly and automatically make any necessary formations. Writing will suffer if the concentration is broken even for a small amount of time.

It is only possible to succeed at a task if we possess the necessary skills, and the ability to spell is obviously a fundamental part of writing. If children are to be competent writers then they must also be competent spellers.

(b) The Necessity for a Structured Learning Programme

There is a very close link between reading and writing but it must never be forgotten that each requires entirely different skills. When a child is reading he is translating visual images into recognisable sounds. He is able to accomplish this task by utilising a combination of textual cues, such as semantic, syntactic and phonic. Spelling, however, relies heavily upon the auditory element and the ability to form the sound into a visually related shape. The only guide a child has in this activity is a knowledge of which letter sequence will probably be appropriate in any given instance. In order to do this he must already be fully aware of the letter patterns which most frequently occur, and are acceptable, in our written language.

It is a mistake to believe that when we are teaching children to read they are simultaneously learning to spell. It is also wrong to assume that a fluent reader will absorb spelling techniques from his reading. In spelling, as with many other areas of education, it is dangerous to rely on incidental learning. Children must have their attention drawn to the regular and frequent letter sequences which occur in our writing system. It must also be remembered that reading relies entirely upon our auditory and visual skills whereas spelling requires us to coordinate these senses with the movements of our hand. This is an important aspect in being able to spell with both speed and accuracy. Not only must children be taught the letter patterns but they must also be given practice in the hand movements which are involved in transcribing these sequences.

With regular and systematic tuition children will eventually discover that the actual task of spelling requires little or no conscious effort on their part. The hand will automatically form the necessary shapes, allowing the writer to concentrate on the ideas he wishes to express. This state of affairs will only be attained through a rational, systematic and structured programme of tuition. Children must be given an awareness of the regularly occurring letter sequences, combined with practice in forming them with the hand. In this way they will internalise the links between sound, shape and hand movements.

Recent research fully supports the idea that spelling techniques must be taught if they are to be completely mastered. Margaret Peters cites the example of a school in which there was no teaching of spelling and at the end of a year 24 per cent of the children had actually deteriorated in their ability to spell. This is an impressive piece of evidence which demonstrates not only the need to instruct children in the skills of spelling, but also proves that the tuition must be continual and consistent if standards are to be maintained or advanced.

Spelling, like any other subject, must be taught in a rational and systematic way. It should be included as a separate, and yet integral, part of any language curriculum and not just considered as a sideline of reading. It is certainly more plausible to suggest that when we are teaching spelling we are also reinforcing phonic work, but it must never be assumed that the converse is also true.

(c) Suggestions for Teaching Spelling

No two teachers work in exactly the same way and similarly no two classes are ever the same. Teaching methods, therefore, must be flexible enough to satisfy the needs and attitudes of both teacher and pupils. However, it is possible to have a broad framework of approach which teachers can adapt to suit their own particular requirements. The most important point is that there must be a clear understanding of what it is we are trying to achieve when we are teaching spelling. From this aim each teacher should plan out a series of steps which will gradually provide the children with all the necessary skills.

Obviously the ultimate aim is that the children will reach a stage whereby they are able to write almost any given word with speed and accuracy. This will only be achieved when they have completely internalised all the conventions of our writing system. Any programme of tuition, therefore, must concentrate on introducing the children to the letter patterns which occur in our writing and also ensure that they practise the hand movements which are associated with each sequence.

Schonell organised the Essential Spelling List into small groups of words which contain the same visual structure and children must have their attention drawn to these patterns. In Group 1 they will encounter the words 'call', 'tall' and 'wall', and the teacher should emphasise the visual element which is common to all the words. Whenever possible it is valuable to indicate that each word contains a small word which they can already spell. In this case it can be shown that each word is simply 'all' with a letter on the front. With encouragement the children should be able to suggest further examples of this pattern which can be written on the board or in a notebook.

The part of the process which involves writing the words should not be neglected because the hand movements must become automatically linked with the audio elements of the word. The best way to achieve this is with repeated practice. The children should write down each of the listed words but without any visual aids. The teacher could perhaps call out the words, or the children could look at each word in their book, concentrate on remembering its visual structure and then write it down without looking at the original. After they have finished writing they can check the accuracy of their attempts. They continue in this manner until the word has been written correctly. Margaret Peters describes this system as a kind of checklist; i.e. look – cover – write – check. The children should be taught the checklist and encouraged to use it whenever they are learning a new word. The use of the checklist will be more successful if the children have already had their attention drawn to the visual pattern of the words.

However, Margaret Peters stresses that words must never be spelt out, either by the teacher or the pupils. The children must become familiar with the visual impact of whole words or letter clusters. A vital skill in spelling is the ability to visualise entire letter sequences and the practice of spelling a word by its individual letters will reduce the speed with which children acquire this technique. For the same reason it is unwise to ask children to copy out words since they will inevitably copy the word letter by letter rather than looking at the whole shape. The children must be trained to look at, and remember, the visual pattern of a word.

The structure of words is interesting and if the teacher can convey an enthusiasm for this area of language then the children will probably adopt a similar attitude and begin to look at words with interest and fascination. The children can be shown that it is often fun to discover that apparently unconnected words do, in fact, share similar roots, and thus the same spelling patterns, such as 'triangle', 'trident', 'trio', and 'tripod'. This can be demonstrated at all levels of difficulty. If we can encourage children to adopt an interest in the structure of words then the teaching of spelling will become considerably easier for all concerned.

As teachers we all have our own techniques and approaches, but as long as we remember what we are trying to achieve then the actual method is less important. If the children are being taught spelling skills within a structured programme that is appropriate to their age, ability and needs, then they will master the necessary techniques.

4 Games and Activities for Consolidation

The initial lesson should be designed to concentrate the childrens' attention upon the letter pattern which is being introduced to them in the word list. For example, in D24 (p. 57) there should be discussion about the 'atch' element which is found in:

match   catch   patch   watch

The children should then be given practice in writing the listed words.

There are many other activities which can be used to consolidate the teaching of spelling. The children will be more enthusiastic if the work is presented in the form of a game, and the element of fun will also help to reinforce what is being learned. However, any games or activities must be such that they continue to highlight the main letter sequences in words. The object of any exercise is to support what is already being actively taught.

(a) Compiling Word Lists

When the spellings from the book have been discussed and understood the children should be asked to suggest other words which belong to the same family. If conducted as a class activity, then write the letter pattern clearly on a chart and pin this to a wall at the children's level. During the week ask the children to write on the chart any words they discover in their reading which contain the relevant sequence. For example, 'bean', 'lean' and 'mean' occur in D18 (p. 52).

In this case the chart should be headed with 'ean' and the list could be started by children whose names contain the pattern, such as Dean and Jean. Local street names and towns should also be included.

A competitive element can be introduced if the listing is done as an individual activity. Give the children a set time, such as the next day or by the end of the week, in which to write down as many words as they can find with the specified pattern.

These activities will encourage the children to concentrate on the structure of words they encounter in their reading. Furthermore, by writing the list they will be repeatedly practising the required hand movements.

(b) Spelling Coordinates

Give each child a sheet of squared paper. Ask the children to number ten squares down and letter ten squares across. Then call out coordinates and ask them to draw a cross in the appropriate square. The crossed squares will eventually form letters. As it becomes more obvious what the letters are going to be the children often enjoy calling out the coordinates themselves.

	a	b	c	d	e	f	g	h	i	j
1										
2		X				X				
3		X				X				
4	X	X	X			X				
5		X				X	X	X		
6		X				X			X	
7		X		X		X	X		X	
8		X	X	X		X		X		
9										
10										

When the letters are complete give the class a time limit in which to list as many words as they can which contain the pattern. Alternatively specify how many words they must write down and ask them to complete their list as quickly as possible.

(c) Words Within Words

Another useful exercise which encourages the children to look carefully at the structure of words is to ask them to look inside a big word and see how many small words they can find.

branch – an, ran, ranch
discontent – is, disc, disco, content, tent, ten

A variation of this activity is to write several words in an unbroken line and ask the children to follow the same procedure, i.e. finding as many small words as possible.

b r i n g o a t e n – bring, oat, ten, ring, in, go, goat, at, ate

(d) Anagrams

Give the children a list of words and explain that the letters of each one must be rearranged into a new word. Clues may be given, either pictorial or verbal, to aid in the discovery of the new word.

mean	becomes	**name**
felt	becomes	**left**
north	becomes	**thorn**

(e) Jumbled Words

Give the children a list of words in which all the letters have been jumbled. Ask the class to discover the original word by placing the letters in their correct order. The words may all contain the same structure or represent a selection of letter patterns which have already been learnt.

kaet – take	or	**isol** – soil
kbrae – brake		**nkip** – pink
ansek – snake		**nrgu** – rung

Some teachers believe that children should never be exposed to letters which are not in a recognised sequence, such as 'cbka'. This attitude is probably justifiable at the early stages of spelling when children are only just beginning to absorb the regularities in our writing system. However, for classes that are conversant with acceptable letter orders it can be an enjoyable exercise to unscramble letters into known words; this can also provide useful practice in sequencing.

(f) The Missing Letter
Write a short passage in which one or more letters are always omitted. Ask the children to discover the letters which are missing.

> The man had his c–at –n but he was still c–ld. He st––d –n the platf–rm and waited f–r the train to c–me. He had been there f–r a 1–ng time.

This activity may appear to be more appropriate as a reading exercise; however, the children are also having to consider what letter will fit suitably into each broken sequence.

(g) Proof Reading
This activity involves the children in finding and then correcting the spelling errors in a passage.

> It <u>wos</u> <u>geting</u> dark as we <u>walkt</u> along the road. My <u>frend</u> started to run but I <u>cood</u> not see very well and <u>befor</u> long she was out of <u>site.</u>

The misspellings should be underlined for children who are at an early stage of learning. This will draw their attention to the incorrect letters and eliminate any confusion.

Children should always be encouraged to check for spelling errors in their own completed written work and a structured exercise is valuable practice in this activity.

(h) Art Work
Spelling activities can also be incorporated into forms of art work. For example, if the class are working on the 'ai' words in D13 (p. 49) then they could make an 'ai' train. Each child draws and cuts out a train carriage and writes an 'ai' word on the side. The carriages are then placed in a line with an engine at the front. Another example is to put a giant plate on the wall and ask each child to make a large chip with a 'ch' word written on it. Stick the chips on the plate. The result is a plateful of 'ch' chips.

5 Testing Spelling

(a) Spelling Tests
The application of a standardised spelling test will give some indication of a child's level of performance within his own particular

age group. Schonell's original tests have been included in this new edition of the book on p. 34. They are in the form of six graded dictation tests. Although it is many years since they were standardised, if they are used sensibly they will still be of help when assessing the children. The tests will give some indication of a child's performance and also provide diagnostic information.

If more detailed information is required about the strengths and weaknesses of a child's spelling then there are recent publications which will be of value. In her *Diagnostic and Remedial Spelling Manual* Margaret Peters provides a series of dictation tests which are relevant to particular age groups. Peters also explains how to categorise spelling mistakes. These categories fall into two main groups, i.e. serious errors and minor errors. For example, two children may each make ten errors in the same dictation test but it does not automatically follow from this result that they are both at the same standard of spelling. One child's mistakes may be reasonable phonic alternatives, which are based upon acceptable and recognised letter sequences; e.g., lait for 'late'. The errors made by the other child, however, may bear little or no resemblance to acceptable letter patterns; e.g., kwik for 'quick'. While the first child has mastered the basic principles of acceptable letter patterns and is well on the way to becoming a competent speller, the second child has much more serious problems which must be diagnosed and corrected. For instance, a child may be experiencing difficulties in auditory or visual perception. Peters analyses the types of errors and likely causes. The book also contains suggestions for remedial action.

Another test is the *Diagnostic Spelling Test* by Denis Vincent and Jenny Claydon. This test measures attainment and indicates any areas of weakness. It tests the children in all the sub-skills which are necessary for good spelling. The areas which are assessed include letter string recognition, proof reading, use of a dictionary and knowledge of serial probability. It also includes a self-concept checklist in which the children are asked to indicate how they see themselves as spellers. It is important to know the image that a child has of himself as a speller. If he has a poor self-image then he is likely to underachieve and he will not make any significant progress until his confidence has been restored.

Apart from standardised tests it is also useful if the children are regularly given an informal spelling test. It would normally be conducted once a week to test the words that have been learnt during the previous few days. Most children will be tested on twelve, sixteen or twenty words, depending on which of the main groups their list has been taken from. Less able children should not be expected to learn this many words. Their test lists should be no more than one or two of the daily units, depending on their age and ability. For these children ten will be the maximum number of words and some will be limited to only three or six words.

A regular spelling test has several values. It provides an incentive for the children to really master the words because success is definite proof of their abilities. A pride in their achievements will encourage them to continue working for the next stage. However, a child's confidence in his spelling abilities will only survive if he is put in a position which allows him to do well. He will fail if the work is too difficult or if the tuition is inadequate. Thus, the work must be at the correct level so that with effort and instruction success is a foregone conclusion.

Weekly tests are also of value to the teacher. As with standardised tests they will reveal any problem areas. A test result may indicate that a large number of children have failed to grasp a particular sequence and the appropriate remedial work can be undertaken. On the other hand it may be only one child who requires extra help with a certain letter pattern. If the results are frequently poor then the level of difficulty probably needs adjusting, or perhaps the lessons can be restructured to give more emphasis to the letter sequences. Under no circumstances must such failing be allowed to continue as this will quickly undermine the attitude and enthusiasm of the children.

Most teachers have developed their own methods for conducting a spelling test but it is advisable to try and avoid the kind of tense atmosphere that is found in examination rooms. This causes some children to become over anxious and reduces the likelihood of their producing their best work. Each word must be spoken clearly and used within the context of a sentence. This will remove the possibility of confusion or mishearing.

A weekly spelling test enables the teacher to discover if the class has learnt the set words. It is also an ideal opportunity for children to prove that they have mastered the skills, and good results will give them confidence in their spelling abilities.

(b) Teaching and Testing Spelling in a Mixed Ability Class
As every teacher of a mixed ability class knows there are certain

problems which must be overcome. This applies no less to spelling than to any other area of the curriculum. Within any class there may be an enormous range of abilities and the children at each level must be given activities that are appropriate to their particular stage of development. For example, in a class of nine year olds some of the children could be capable of learning the lists in Group 5, whereas other children may not be ready to progress beyond Group 1. For most of the class Group 3 would be about the right level. However, this will not be the case in all classes of this age. There may not be such an extreme range of abilities and the children would be working on Groups 2, 3 and 4. It is necessary to assess the levels of ability and structure the work accordingly.

The supplementary tasks must also be appropriate to the needs of the children. The most able childen should be expected to undertake more difficult examples of the games and activities which are suggested in the section on p. 11; e.g., complex proof reading exercises. The less able children will be far less independent in their learning. A remedial child who is studying the words in Group 1 will need more assistance, and his activities could involve no more than writing and illustrating short lists of visually related words.

If all the children are expected to work at the same pace and level then at least one section of the class will not be developing at an acceptable rate. The more able children will become bored and dissatisfied if the work is too easy. They will also be prevented from making any substantial progress. However, if the work is aimed at these children, then the slower ones are likely to fail because they are being denied the opportunity to pass through the intermediate stages that are essential for steady development. Each child should be progressing at a rate that is compatible with his needs and abilities.

Ideally, each class member should be working at his own individual level, but unfortunately, this is usually impractical. The more convenient method is to arrange the class into two or three ability groups, as mentioned above.

Standardised test results can be used as a means of assessment when deciding which level of difficulty is most suitable for a particular child. The Graded Dictations (p. 87) will give an indication of a child's attainment, as will the published tests referred to on p. 15. Some teachers will prefer to rely on a combination of informal tests and their own professional judgement. Whatever method of selection is used it is always advisable to retain some movement between the

17

groups. A child experiencing difficulties will benefit from a short spell at a lower level and a child who is making good progress may be ready for a higher level.

There are difficulties associated with ability grouping, such as all the children making different demands at the same time. These problems can be partially avoided by instigating an organised routine, so that the children know exactly what their group should be doing while the others are being attended to. For instance, while one group is being given instruction on a new list the others could be practising their previous spellings with the look – cover – write – check routine. Children will usually cooperate if they know what is expected of them.

There should also be a regular routine for conducting the weekly spelling test. One method is to test each group separately while the rest of the class are quietly involved in other activities until it is their turn to be tested. It is also possible to test all the groups at one sitting, by calling out one word at a time from each list; the children write down those words that are applicable to them. Children will usually respond well to an organised system; if they fully understand their part in the proceedings then the inherent problems will be reduced to a minimum.

6 Vocabulary and Dictionary Work

(a) Vocabulary Activities

Vocabulary work can be derived from the spelling lists in this book, even when all the words are known to the children. It is useful to ask the children to give an accurate definition of each of the words in their weekly list. Any variations in usage can be demonstrated by placing the words within the context of a sentence. For example, it should be shown that the word 'club' in Group 2 can be used in several ways; i.e. a stick used as a weapon, the action of hitting with a stick, equipment used in golf, a group of people who meet regularly, the building they meet in, and one of the suits in a pack of cards. It is often fun to see how many differences can be found in the use and meaning of just one word.

At first children will find it difficult to give clear definitions, but it is surprising how quickly they become adept at this activity. The exercise has two main values. First, they are being encouraged to articulate their thoughts without ambiguity. Second, they are having

18

to analyse the use and meaning of words. This will help them to develop a greater awareness of words, which will indirectly benefit their spelling abilities.

Occasionally the lists may contain words that are unknown to the children and these must be carefully explained with examples of their usage. This will occur more frequently in classes which include children for whom English is a second language since they are often uncertain of even relatively commonplace words.

When the words have been discussed the children could then be asked to compose a sentence for each word. This ensures that they are able to use the vocabulary correctly and also gives practice in writing the words within a context. Younger or less able children may not be able to accomplish much written work but they can illustrate each word with a simple drawing. Some children benefit from being given incomplete sentences and asked to fill in the missing word with an appropriate one from their list.

(b) Dictionary Activities

Dictionary work can be closely identified with spelling skills because both rely on the ability to understand the structure of words. However, before a child can use a dictionary he must be completely familiar with the concept of alphabetical order; this can be achieved with the appropriate activities.

When the children are competent at the initial skill of alphabetical sequencing they can then be introduced to the various uses of this system. They usually enjoy discovering that their names are arranged alphabetically in the class register, and the use of short indexes in simple reference books is also a valuable exercise. At a later stage children often find it fun to look up the names of friends and relatives in a local telephone didrectory.

The words in the spelling lists can be found in the dictionary and the meanings read aloud. It is often interesting to compare the definitions given in the discussion to those in the dictionary.

All these activities, however, involve the ability to look up a word for which the spelling is already known, but we also use a dictionary to discover how a word is spelt. Children must, therefore, be shown how to find a word when they are unsure of the spelling. They must be taught to use their judgement of what is the probable structure of the unknown word, and if the first attempt is wrong then they must consider what would be a likely alternative and check for this in the

19

dictionary. One aspect of this skill is the ability to find a word when only the initial letters are known. Children can practise this task by being given just the first two or three letters of a word, plus the definition; e.g., str . . . a small river. They must then use the dictionary to complete the word.

There are two distinct skills involved in using a dictionary. One is looking for the meaning of a word when the spelling is known and the other is the ability to find a word without being sure of the spelling. Children should be given practice in both techniques.

7 The Dictations

(a) The Value of Dictation Exercises

The dictation passages are intended to be used as an integral part of the teaching programme. Each passage includes a selection of words from three or four consecutive sets of words and should be given to the children when the work on these lists has been completed. For example, the first dictation should be used when the children have learnt the three sets of words in D1 (p. 42).

Up to this point most of the words will have been taught in isolation. Not only do the dictations help to reinforce the work but they also enable the children to experience the words being used within a context. This simulates the process of writing which will be expected from them at a later stage. When they are writing freely they will use the words within a context and also spell them from memory. The dictation exercises require them to use both these skills, but within a practice situation.

A proficiency in writing is also, to some extent, related to the speed at which it is accomplished, and dictations encourage children to write quickly and automatically. They soon discover that prolonged hesitations can result in the undesirable position of being left behind. During dictation they are forced to write spontaneously and to trust their instinctive hand movements.

The possibility of becoming muddled is also a deterrent against the children allowing themselves to be distracted. They know that they must continually listen and pay close attention. This has the effect of developing their powers of concentration.

As with a weekly spelling test, the dictation passages are also a useful means of giving the children confidence in their own abilities. During free writing activities they will often ask for a spelling rather

20

than risk failing on their own. However, because this help is not available in a dictation they have no alternative but to trust their own judgement. Therefore, dictations are an excellent way of proving to children that they can write without constant assistance. If the level of difficulty is correct then they will succeed. This will give them a feeling of pride and confidence which will be transferred into other areas of their work.

The results of a dictation exercise should also be used to diagnose any particular problems. There should be an awareness of the two main categories of errors which are discussed on p. 15, i.e. serious errors and minor errors. If a child consistently makes serious errors then he requires remedial spelling tuition at a level as basic as the lists in Group 1. The dictations will also give an indication of any minor problems which are being experienced by groups or individuals. Appropriate work should be provided once the problem has been diagnosed.

(b) Techniques for Conducting a Dictation Exercise

During most written exercises children are able to determine their own rate of work. However, in a dictation it is someone else who controls the pace and this factor often results in a sense of panic. This is most likely to occur when the children are given their first few dictations, but if the teacher responds sympathetically then they will gradually gain in confidence and their fears will subside.

The entire passage should be read to the children before they begin writing. This will give them an understanding of the story they are about to write. The speed at which the passage is read should be determined by the age and ability of the children. If the reading is too fast then some children will be panicked into making unnecessary mistakes. If it is too slow then they could lose concentration, especially if the pause between each phrase is too long. The speed must be judged according to the performance of the children, but a suitable pace can only be achieved if all the children involved are of a similar level of ability. If a dictation from Group 5 is used, for instance, than all the participant children should be capable of this standard.

At first the children may ask for spellings, but they must be told to attempt the words on their own. They should also be discouraged from using rubbers as this will slow them down and cause them to become muddled. They should be given the punctuation marks, but it is up to the discretion of the teacher as to whether they are also informed when to use a capital letter. It may be assumed that older children are capable of applying these correctly on their own.

When the writing has been completed the entire passage should be read through again so that the children can check for any missing words. They should also be given enough time to look for, and correct, any obvious spelling errors.

(c) Dictation Exercises in a Mixed Ability Class

In a mixed ability class the children should already be working in spelling groups according to their level of attainment. Some children will be working from Groups 1 or 2, whereas others could be studying from Groups 5 and 6. In each case the relevant dictation must be used. The book has been structured in such a way that the passages and spelling lists are totally compatible. For every three or four word lists there is always a corresponding dictation passage which incorporates the set words. Children should only be given the dictation which is directly related to the lists they have been learning. Therefore, if there are three ability groups then it will be necessary to read three dictations. For instance, in a class of ten year olds some of the children may have learnt the words in D19 and they must be given Dictation 19. Others may have been studying D34 and in this case Dictation 34 should be used. The same procedure should be followed for the highest group.

The length and vocabulary of each passage is designed to meet the needs of the ability group for which it is intended, and the passages will fail to serve their purpose if the correct dictation is not used.

As explained in the section on spelling tests, it is important that a measure of success is ensured, otherwise chidren will lose confidence and interest. If this is allowed to happen then it will ultimately affect their performance in other written work. However, if each ability group has mastered the necessary word structures, then they will find no difficulty with the dictation exercises.

It is advisable that the routine suggested for testing spelling is also adopted when reading the dictations. While one group is receiving their dictation passage the other children could be gainfully employed. The general approach of the teacher, and the speed at which the passage is read, will need to be adjusted according to the abilities of the children who are completing the dictation.

22

8 Summary of the Main Points

Research has shown that children will not simply absorb spelling skills from their reading, but must be taught the necessary techniques. They must be given systematic tuition which draws their attention to the structure of words and the regularities which occur in our spelling system. A programme of spelling lists, dictations and consolidating activities will provide them with the opportunity to acquire the essential skills successfully. However, in order to derive the greatest benefit, the lessons should be approached in a way that is appropriate for the age and ability of the children.

It is hoped that the notes in this introduction will be of assistance to teachers and give them a springboard from which to devise their own activities and support work.

9 Further Reading

Teachers Books

Peters, M. L., *Spelling: Caught or Taught?*, Routledge and Kegan Paul, 1967.

Peters, M. L. and Cripps, C. C., *Appraisal of Current Spelling Materials: A Consumers Guide*, Centre for the Teaching of Reading, University of Reading, 1980.

Torbe, M., *Teaching Spelling*, Ward Lock Educational, 1977. A very useful and concise guide.

Pupils Books

Schonell, F. J., *Essential Spelling List*, Macmillan Education, 1932.

Schonell, F. J. and F. C., *Essential Read–Spell*, Macmillan Education, Revised 1980.

Hornsby, B., *Alpha to Omega*, Heinemann, 1976.

Ballance, D. and H., *Nelson Spelling*, Nelson, 1977.

Peters, M. L. and Cripps, C. C., *Word Bank Project*, Macmillan Education, 1978.

Peters, M. L. and Cripps, C. C., *Catch Words*, Harcourt, Brace and Jovanovich, 1978.

Sadler, B. R. and Page, E. G., *Blackwells Spelling Workshop*, Blackwell, 1976. A large and thorough pack of cards and other teaching materials. Relevant to remedial use.

Tests

Peters, M. L., *Diagnostic and Remedial Spelling Manual*, Macmillan Education, 1975. This is as much a guide to teaching spelling using the look–cover–write–check routine as a test. A vital book for reference and for practical use in the classroom using the accompanying diagnostic record sheets.

Vincent, D. and Claydon, J., *Diagnostic Spelling Test*, NFER-Nelson, 1982. The best group spelling test currently available which provides standardised scores from its seven sub-tests which are useful for teaching children and remedying their problems.

INTRODUCTION TO THE FIRST EDITION

1 Compilation of List of Everyday Words for English Children

The suggestions on the teaching and testing of spelling set out in the following pages have resulted, in a large measure, from an extensive investigation into Disability in Spelling amongst London Elementary School Children.[1] The Spelling Lists and Graded Dictation Reviews, which accompany the text, are, in part, material which was used for remedial work with backward spellers. At the time of the research no lists of words exactly suited to the purpose were to be obtained. It was not possible simply to adapt the spelling lists of American investigators because there are definite differences in vocabulary content of American and English children.[2] For example, American lists contain a number of such words as cooky, candy, sled, cute, creek, ranch, gotten, gasoline, railroad, dollar, words which an English Elementary School child rarely, if ever, uses. Moreover, the spelling of words differs on each side of the Atlantic, as is seen in these examples from American texts, center, labor, catalog, check (cheque), offense, fulfill, skillful, mustache, mold. Hence it was decided to select, grade and group all the common words that English Elementary School children should be able to spell.

In the selection of the words a debt must be acknowledged to Dr

---

[1] Carried out under the guidance of Professor Cyril Burt, who gave invaluable help and advice both in the conduct of the enquiry and the interpretation of results.

[2] Mention must here be made of a very useful conribution by Dr Boyd of Glasgow University. For particulars see Boyd, W., *Measuring Devices in Composition, Spelling and Arithmetic*, Harrap and Co., 1924.

Horn's publication *A Basic Writing Vocabulary*.[1] This author, aided by a grant from the Commonwealth Fund enabling him to obtain adequate, skilled assistance for the examination of data, compiled, from literary, personal and business writings of adults, involving 5 136 000 words, a list of the 10 000 words most commonly used in writing. From these, printed with figures to denote frequency of use, and signs to show words found in the Thorndike List,[2] and from an extensive survey of children's written English, it was possible to select a body of 3 200 words that would form an adequate spelling vocabulary for an average Elementary School pupil.

The words were first graded into six major groups of increasing number. Their actual distribution was based on the principle that the child should be taught the word when he wants to write it. The grading was checked by experienced teachers and by reference to written material of children of ages 7–12. These tentative lists, divided into smaller units to facilitate testing on successive days, were given to children in schools of average social grade. From the results a fairly reliable estimate of the relative difficulty of the words within each group was obtained. The next step involved grouping the words in small sets according to common structural elements, for reliable experimental evidence shows that learning words so grouped produces ten to twenty per cent greater efficiency in both immediate and delayed recall, than when words are learned in indiscriminate lists. This method could not be employed exclusively throughout; with the lists of more difficult words, grouping according to context and according to common error was occasionally employed. Finally, from time to time, as use and experience dictated, minor modifications were made in the allocation of words and the positions of small groups. The final lists were only evolved after over a year's trial and consideration.

2 Use of the Essential Spelling List in Schools

The Essential Spelling List contains in all six word lists, designated as

---

[1] Horn, Ernest., *A Basic Writing Vocabulary : 10,000 Words Most Commonly Used in Writing*, University of Iowa Monographs in Education, First Series, No. 4, Iowa City, 1926.
[2] Thorndike, E. L., *The Teachers' Word Book*, Teachers' College, Columbia University, New York, 1921.

Groups 1, 2, 3, 4, 5, 6 respectively, and containing a total of 3 200 words. The number of words in each group increases from approximately 400 in the first to 600 in the sixth. The groups themselves are definitely of increasing difficulty, while the words within each group become, in the main, successively harder. They include common words which Elementary School children use in writing, and all of which children of average intelligence should be able to spell correctly at the age of 13.

It is intended that the words should constitute the basic material for curricula requirements in the Elementary School. If a child has mastered these he can spell most of the words he wishes to write and 80–90 per cent of those found in the majority of books and newspapers. It is intended, too, that each Group should provide words sufficient for the spelling lessons of a school year. Although the basis of both selection and grading has been frequency of child usage, yet in all cases the lists should be sparingly supplemented with words of local significance, composition requirements and specific experiences. It is not intended that a particular Group should be used with a particular class, or that it is only suitable to children of a particular age. Use of a Group will vary considerably with the intellectual calibre of the class. Selection of Group will best be determined by the discerning class teacher himself, but results indicate that the following assignments are most suitable:

	Number of Words	Age	Standard
GROUP 1	396	7	(I)
GROUP 2	456	8	(II)
GROUP 3	544	9	(III)
GROUP 4	576	10	(IV)
GROUP 5	600	11	(V)
GROUP 6	600	12	(VI)

The words have been arranged in small units of a day's assignment, varying from three in the first to five in the final list. Furthermore, in most instances the fourth unit contains words similar in structure to those studied on the three previous days. The reproduction of a specimen set from Group 3 better exemplifies the underlying principles of construction.

26

team	**slave**	**front**	
steam	**shave**	**month**	
scream	**grave**	**Monday**	
gleam	**cape**	**ton**	
shape	**treat**	**won**	**wonder**

It will be noticed that there are only four units in a set, as it was thought that the fifth day might profitably be spent in reviewing all words of the preceding four days' assignments. It must be reiterated that it is not intended to lay down hard and fast rules of procedure, for, so different are the achievements and the capacities of children in spelling, that procedure must depend, not only upon the calibre of the class, but upon the nature of the individual; it must be adaptable, at first being determined by the child's present requirements, later changed by future developments.

3 Principles in Teaching Spelling

In the following paragraphs the most important factors in the teaching of spelling are briefly discussed. They are mainly those which experimental findings, practical classroom experience and the investigations into spelling disability have demonstrated as being of most value. The principles enumerated below determined the method of construction in the accompanying spelling lists and graded dictation reviews.

The first essential is that children should be taught words which they use frequently in their written work and that they should not waste time learning words which they seldom use. The class teacher's motto should be 'concentrate on common words'. Although this principle has been a characteristic of curricula content for the past decade, there are still some who believe that a child should be able to spell the words in the literature he reads. Most children can read many words a year or more before they can spell them. There is a definite difference between spelling vocabulary and reading vocabulary; there obtains, more with younger than with older children, what Professor Burt terms 'a period of orthographic latency'.[1] Adherence to this principle does not, of course, preclude the child from learning other words through incidental reading and

---

[1] Burt, C., *Mental and Scholastic Tests*, P. S. King and Son, 1926, p. 288.

the use of a dictionary, but it does ensure that the time devoted to spelling lessons is employed to its maximum advantage.

This leads us to a consideration of the proportion of time to be allotted to drill and individual methods. Some teachers, reacting too far from the unpedagogical mass teaching of earlier days, discountenance drill as a monotonous, mechanical method which the child dislikes. This contention, however, is too sweeping, for with young children, up to the age of about nine, there is ample evidence that 'rhythmic repetition' is psychologically sound. As Sir Percy Nunn says, 'the child's repertory of accomplishments is narrowly limited, he loves, therefore, to repeat the familiar because he gets from it the fullest sense of effective self-assertion.'[1] This is the stage when pride in individual achievement and mastery by constant reiteration are at their strongest, hence teachers should take full advantage of these tendencies to fix fundamentals which later must function automatically.

Although drill methods are indispensable in junior classes, they should be supplemented, especially with brighter children, by individual approaches. For pupils of ages 10 and 11 the spelling lesson can almost exclusively take the form of organised study supervision. This latter point has been admirably demonstrated, generally by Dr Washbourne in the Winnetka Schools[2] and specifically by Miss Barnard[3] in a carefully planned experiment on the teaching of spelling. The last-named paired children, ten and eleven years old, of poor spelling ability with those of good spelling ability. From individually assigned lists each child learnt at home a number of words which his partner dictated and corrected next day. Any errors were included in his next day's assignment. Statistical comparison with other groups of children of the same age and ability, who learnt only by class methods, revealed a distinct superiority in favour of the individual procedure.

The third principle concerns the actual presentation of words. Spelling material will be more readily and permanently mastered if

---

[1] Nunn, Sir T. Percy, *Education, Its Data and First Principles*, Edward Arnold and Co., 1930, p. 71.

[2] See *Report on Survey of Winnetka Schools*, Washbourne, Vogel and Gray Public Schools Publishing Co., Bloomington, Illinois, 1924.

[3] Barnard, Agnes M., *An Experimental Study in Spelling*, Supplement to the *Scottish Educational Journal*, June, 1931. No. 5.

words are grouped in small units according to some rational plan. Briefly, four types of grouping appear to be useful:

(a) associating words of similar auditory and visual elements as in:

power
shower
tower

(b) associating words of similar visual, but slightly dissimilar auditory elements as in:

stove
glove
prove

For the child who is prone to phonetic analogies, drill with this group is often an effective antidote.

(c) a combination of grouping according to both common elements and context; e.g.,

needle
thimble
button
cotton

(d) grouping according to a common silent letter as in:

knee	or	comb
kneel		crumb
knock		thumb
knob		climb

If the words are taught separately, or as part of a lesson on various silent letters, the children find difficulty, not so much in remembering that there is a silent letter in the word, but in recalling the correct one. I reproduce below two examples from my own investigation, the first, the case of a girl who wrote 'dept' for 'debt', the second that of a boy who put 'gnuckle' for 'knuckle', after an indiscriminate presentation of silent letter words one of which was 'gnaw'. It is perhaps prudent to deal with one silent letter in a lesson, allowing some time to elapse before another is studied.

Perhaps the greatest value of grouping lies in the fact that it gives the child experience with families of common letter combinations which, when familiar, will transfer, at first consciously, later uncons-

29

ciously, to unlearned words of similar structure. There does not seem to be any doubt that with some children this process functions unconsciously; they analyse and synthesise without conscious effort and can read and spell almost any word that is put before them. With a large percentage of children, however, it is advisable to draw attention to the rational elements in the language. It was constantly noticed that where a child erroneously spelled words such as 'stitch' and 'church', drill in groups containing the troublesome consonantal diagraph at once dispersed the difficulty.

Furthermore, intentional grouping obviates the confusions that sometimes occur through a chance listing of words. An example, selected from a long list of errors due to this factor, clarifies the point. A class of girls learnt a list of words containing 'channel' and 'canal'. Chance association of these forms in the same assignment produced, with almost half the class, confusion in the spelling of the two words. These errors persisted for several weeks. Had 'channel' been intentionally placed with such similar forms as 'flannel' and 'funnel', and had 'canal' been presented in its appropriate group in a later lesson, confusion would have been minimised.

Lastly, words grouped with respect to similarity of constituent elements form excellent basic material for reading lessons and exercises in speech training. Defective pronunciation is a considerable source of misspelling, and a method of teaching which provides for repetition of common sound combinations, spoken as well as written, is making a dual contribution.

A maxim, extremely important yet often ignored in the teaching of spelling, is that of presenting a few words at a time. It is infinitely more effective to give, four times a week in five to ten minute periods, three, four or five words per day, the actual number being dependent on the ability of the children, than to attempt to teach twelve to twenty words, in one period of twenty or thirty minutes. The adult will see the fallacy of the latter procedure if he notes the accuracy and permanency of his recall in what is for him a comparable task, namely that of learning the spelling and meaning of sets of forty unfamiliar French or German words *en masse* at one presentation, or in sections at several sittings. It is mainly for this reason that the words in the Groups have been distributed into small study units. Moreover, the child likes to feel that he has completed and mastered a section of his work; he is slightly dismayed by the formidable task which a long list of words presents.

30

The actual method of presenting words to juniors is best left to the ingenuity of the class teacher. There are, however, certain vital points of procedure that might be noted. It is essential that the child should attend to the parts of a word as well as to the whole. Development of an analytic and synthetic attitude in word observation will assist him later, when spelling lessons are almost exclusively individual activities. Experimental studies in perception show that the backward speller is definitely inferior to the normal speller in his attack upon words. In the initial stages, therefore, how to study will be as important as what to study. In furtherance of this point, it is of doubtful psychological validity to alter the pattern of a word by marking the hard spots in colour or underlining likely sources of error. Research reveals that it is necessary to draw attention to catch parts of words, but it is a hindrance to introduce devices that will lead to a distortion of the normal visual image.

All channels of ingress should be employed in learning. It is by combination of visual, auditory, articulatory (involving accurate pronunciation) and grapho-motor impressions that the spelling of words is firmly fixed in the memory. Two devices, one introducing supplementary kinaesthetic and the other tactile sensory impressions, can often be profitably utilised. In the former the child traces the word in large letters, either in the air with his fingers, or on the desk with the unsharpened end of his pencil. In the latter, he runs his finger tips over the word, the letters of which have been cut out in sandpaper or in velvet pile.[1]

In both immediate and delayed tests, words are more efficiently recalled when learnt in column form than when studied in phrases, sentences or paragraps. Moreover, ability to transfer the spelling of words to new contexts is not favoured by the latter method. Of course learned words should be integrated with other material as soon as possible. Children should be encouraged to use them in composition or to embody them in English exercises.

The practice of teaching homonyms together is, as both classroom and experimental results demonstrate, a faulty one. Words of the same sound but different spelling are soonest mastered if taught separately. Certainly with such pairs as 'there' and 'their', which appear in the child's vocabulary at about the same time, one can

---

[1] This is perhaps necessary with only a few individuals who experience unusual difficulty in learning to spell.

introduce explanatory phrases to help. Suitable grouping – 'there, where, here' – will materially assist the child. Needless confusion is aroused by associating pairs of homonyms, particularly when one of them is foreign to the child, in all probability a word that he will not want to use for several years. The following example aptly illustrates this point. It was observed that several children in a class often spelled 'leaf' as 'lief'. Enquiry revealed that the two words had been previously presented together in an English lesson. Many similar examples of homonymous confusion, which might have been avoided, could be cited. Homonyms have purposely been kept apart in the spelling lists reproduced below.

The spelling lesson need not be uninteresting if it is successfully motivated and linked up with the interests of the children. Play activities should be utilised, for play is instinctive in its appeal during childhood, and experience shows that it is one of the most effective forces in stimulating effort and developing useful habits. In both class revision and when pairs of pupils test one another's home assignments, playway methods are excellent. For example, children might be asked to write two derivatives of, or three words similar in structure to, those they were required to memorise. Or again, words might be presented as jumbled letters, a device which concentrates attention on relative letter order and minimises recall by solely auditory means. Thus the teacher might write previously learned words on the blackboard in the following form:

tbture (butter)
ifteh (thief)

the scholars being required to write them correctly.

With older children, whose assignment has been six or eight words, revision can frequently be combined with the day's English lesson. The class teacher might simply say, 'See who can write, in ten minutes, the most interesting composition of five lines, including the words you learnt last night.' Powers of English construction and imagination, as well as those of orthography, are thus given scope.

Finally frequent reviews are an indispensable factor in the spelling programme. Weekly and monthly revisions, not necessarily by testing, consolidate progress made and repay initial expenditure of time and energy. Children should be encouraged to keep a small note book, with an alphabetical index, in which they record errors made in composition and during specific lessons in the subject. In addition to introducing an element of play, the idea of entering words under their respective initial letters is a means of familiarising children with dictionaries. It may be observed in passing that every pupil should possess a small dictionary which he can readily use. Dictionary work is definitely an aid to orthography for it inculcates a desire for correct spelling and emphasises visual form and relative letter order of words.

To meet the need for revision, Graded Dictation Reviews have been constructed from the Essential Spelling List. Considerable care has been bestowed upon these, each of which is based upon the words found in three or four consecutive small sets. The teacher is at liberty to use them as he thinks fit. The prose might be written on the blackboard and the children allowed to study it for several minutes. On the other hand it might be emphasised simply for periodical test purposes, the results of which pupils could record on progress charts. The Graded Reviews provide practice in listening to dictation and eleminate the injurious effects that sometimes accrue from repeated use of difficult unseen passages. Discouragement and initial errors which often persist are both likely products of the unseen dictation.

4 Testing Spelling

We are all aware that continuous testing and measuring will not in themselves produce growth, but we should also all be aware that without adequate testing and measuring we can neither diagnose deficiency nor indicate progress. Hence it is important that we should have, when we need them, instruments that will assist us in comparing achievements and in diagnosing disability. For the teacher, these instruments are carefully compiled, standardised tests. They enable him to compare children in various ages from different classes and different schools. In spelling, three separate tests are helpful in this respect:

(a) Graded Spelling Tests;
(b) Graded Dictation Tests;
(c) Graded Irregular and Regular Word Tests.

Of the first type, probably the most useful to English teachers and investigators is Dr Burt's Graded Vocabulary Test. Judicious selection of words, careful gradation of age assignments and accurate standardisation have made it a most reliable and indicative measure of a child's spelling achivement.[1]

In addition to a discontinuous test, it is advisable to obtain an estimate of a child's ability to write continuous material from dictation. Not only has this form of test the obvious advantage over an isolated list of words, in that it is less artificial, but it also reveals particular errors characteristic of many classroom writing activities. Hence a set of Graded Dictation Tests are given below.[2] Three steps were observed in their construction. Firstly a number of words for each age group from 7 to 12 was selected. The relative difficulties of these were determined by testing, the results facilitating the elimination of both very easy and very hard words. The next step was to embody the remaining words in each group, with the aid of simple connecting material, in a series of continuous passages. These, too, were submitted to preliminary trials which in turn produced modifications. The standardised compilations which finally emerged from the initial test sheets are as follows:

Graded Dictation Tests

Test A

The ship came over the deep blue sea
To bring all kinds of things for me,
A little toy box and a pretty red train.
O thank you good ship, please do come again.

Test B

I spent four days at a farm in the country. I had such a nice time because the people were so good to me. One night we set out for a walk to the old church; before we had gone half way, however, it began to rain so we had to turn back.

Test C

While the weather was fine my aunt and uncle took me out for the day. They paid for me to go on the steamer. The river was very pretty and it was a change to see boats instead of cars. After we had passed

---

[1] Burt, C., *Mental and Scholastic Tests*, P. S. King and Son, Third ed., 1927. See pp. 287–288 for Instructions; pp. 354 and 402 for Test and Norms. Reprinted separately in *A Handbook of Tests*, P. A. King and Son, 1927, p. 16.

[2] Jointly compiled with Dr G. Sleight, Headmaster of Hamilton Road School, Birmingham, to whom I am indebted for the performance norms.

the bridge we caught sight of the mountain, which looked so grand that we bought a picture of it.

Test D

It was a beautiful day, and a large crowd attended the sports; many ladies and gentlemen waited at the entrance to the field for hours before the gates opened. The boys and girls came by special train. It was a wonderful success and our school won the jumping and many races. We were pleased with the result and spent a very happy time.

Test E

The engine stopped, the vessel drifted from her course; the captain believed that it was impossible to prevent the boat from being wrecked. It was certain they could go no further, neither would their supply of provisions last long even if they reached the island. Unless the ship they had recently passed came to assist them they must lose their lives.

Test F

The secretary called a meeting of the association to discuss the important question of Empire Free Trade. The majority of the members agreed that it would probably be good for business to organise and develop trade with the colonies. Others put forward the argument that it would increase expense to tax foreign goods. After some debate it was decided to form a committee to consider the possibility of sending a representative to the national conference.

The instructions for giving the passages are quite simple. Select a test which is approximately suitable to the individual or the bulk of the individuals under consideration. Read aloud the entire paragraph to give the testees an indication of its meaning. Then dictate in phrases of three or four words, repeating each phrase after an interval of two seconds.

Scoring is as follows:

1 Mark all words wrongly spelled. Calculate the number of errors. If a child has more then twenty-five errors, the test is deemed too difficult for him and his performance is deduced from an easier test.
2 By reference to Table I, find the positive score equivalent to the number of errors.
3 By reference to Table II, find the equivalent mental age from the positive mark.

35

TABLE I GRADED DICTATION TESTS
Errors in Test

A	B	C	D	E	F	Equivalent positive score
17	24					1
16	23					2
15	22					3
14	21					4
13	20	25				5
12	19	24				6
11	18	23				7
10	17	22				8
10	16	21				9
9	15	20				10
8	14	19				11
7	13	18				12
7	12	17	25			13
6	11	16	24			14
6	10	15	23			15
5	9	14	21			16
5	8	13	19			17
4	7	12	18	25		18
4	6	11	16	24		19
3	6	10	15	22		20
3	5	9	13	20		21
2	4	8	12	18		22
1	3	7	11	17	25	23
0	2	6	10	15	23	24
	2	5	8	13	21	25
	1	4	7	11	19	26
	0	3	5	9	17	27
		2	4	8	15	28
		1	3	6	13	29
		0	2	5	11	30
			1	4	9	31
			0	3	7	32
				1	5	33
				0	3	34
					1	35

TABLE II   GRADED DICTATION TESTS
(Averages in terms of positive score)

Age	Boys	Girls
7	14.2	15.5
8	19.5	20.9
9	24.2	25.4
10	26.0	28.2
11	28.2	29.0
12	29.2	30.0
13	30.0	31.0

The Irregular and Regular Word Lists are intended primarily for use in obtaining a comparative estimate of the child's ability to spell phonetic and non-phonetic words. The Irregular list is composed solely of words containing such pitfalls as silent letters, double letters, indeterminate vowels and confusing vowel digraphs. The Regular Test material, on the other hand, is a collection of units having a high degree of correspondence between audible sound and visible symbol. The accompanying printed lists are the most suitable selections from extensive preliminary trials with approximately 200 words of each type. To facilitate testing they have been arranged in order of increasing difficulty, based on 700 spellings of each word. It should be noted that tests 1A and 1B are essentially diagnostic tests for use with backward spellers of all ages. They are not really effective as attainment tests for pupils beyond the age of 10 years.

Finally results from all tests discussed in the foregoing paragraphs provide, in addition to measures of attainment, concrete examples of errors in carefully selected material. This is not their least valuable contribution, for a careful analysis of a child's errors provides, for the class teacher, available suggestive data that will be of assistance in the prevention of future misspellings. Are the errors mainly omissions? Is there a tendency to transpose, revealing slovenly visual perception? Is substitution common, especially in vowels, indicating lack of auditory discrimination? Are the errors further distorted by mispronunciation? These are some of the questions which will arise and must be answered if children are to be helped with their spelling difficulties.

TABLE III
Test 1A   Spelling. Irregular Words

Age	No. of correct words	
	Averages	
	Boys	Girls
7	22.7	25.3
8	25.2	29.8
9	32.8	36.8
10	40.0	42.5
11	43.3	45.8
12	45.5	47.7
13	47.0	50.5

TABLE IV
Test 1B   Spelling. Regular Words

Age	No. of correct words	
	Averages	
	Boys	Girls
7	32.2	34.7
8	35.2	38.2
9	41.0	43.6
10	46.1	47.0
11	50.2	50.8
12	51.3	52.0
13	52.2	53.9

Test 1A
Spelling. Irregular Words

was cow one car box
toy put out cry ask

class butter blue light wished
merry again world chase hardly

because spoil climb engine ribbon
instead cloudy sudden laugh built

coffee curtain traffic purple orchard
quickly poetry juice telegram southern

gallery dodge stitch awful suitable
opposite coloured special neither stomach

frequently scissors approach separate scarcely
expense bicycle extremely initials receipt

Test 1B
Spelling. Regular Words

top wet pig peg tub
sit mud rod hop van

thing winter belong left bunch
start oldest march storm thunder

remind chapter trusting repay driven
reporter sung planted whenever growing

latest understand punish pretend contented inviting
membership providing remember situated

devoting unbroken refreshment problem visited employer
extended adventure splendid congratulate

unexpected establishing promotion instructed ventilated
representation gratitude magnificent prescription inconvenient

Test 1B is of considerable diagnostic value, for it gives an indication of the degree of an examinee's mastery of common standard combinations such as 'ch', 'st', 'th', 'ng', and 'tion'. It yields, too, a measure of his power of phonetic analysis, more particularly with regular vowel formations, and provides a check on purity of pronunciation and capacity for syllabification. Evidence of faulty functioning of these factors is seen in the errors of a girl, age 10, who wrote 'remeber' (remember), 'contened' (contended), 'mebership' (membership), and 'incovenent' (inconvenient).

The Norms in Table III, and Table IV, were derived from testing 1 400 children, ages 7–13, with approximately equal numbers of each sex.

Acknowledgements

The author wishes to express his gratitude to teachers and children who have contributed towards the preparation of this book, and particularly to Headteachers of numerous schools of the London County Council and to Miss H. Smith and Mr G. H. Thurley of the Tottenham Urban District Council. He also owes a debt to Professor Cyril Burt for fruitful suggestions regarding the text, and above all to his wife for constant encouragement and continuous constructive assistance with the entire material.

THE ESSENTIAL SPELLING LIST

The letters D1, D2, D3 etc. indicate the group of words to which the Graded Dictations on pp. 87–101 apply. For example, the three sets of words given in D1 on p. 42 are reviewed in Dictation 1 on p. 87.

GROUP 1

D1

man	get	run
can	wet	gun
ran	let	sun

met   fun   ant

red	did	hot
bed	hid	not
fed	lid	blot

spot   led   lip

had	bud	tell
sad	mud	fell
glad	rug	bell

dug   well   has

D2

pin	pet	top
tin	set	stop
win	leg	shop

peg   dog   tip

ill	bat	nut
hill	that	cut
will	bag	but

rag   fill   shut

rub	sit	yes
tub	bit	yet
dust	dig	pen
	open fog pig	

D3

look	kill	cap
book	till	tap
took	mill	clap
	cook trap still	

all	men	here
ball	ten	where
fall	then	there
	small egg when	

end	sing	good
send	king	wood
mend	thing	foot
	boot lend them	

D4

ring	old	call
bring	hold	tall
spring	told	wall
	gold bold calling	

him	was	her
his	wash	she
this	want	they
	sum drum what	

43

see		six		by
tree		fix		cry
been		box		try
	sky	sweet	fox	

D5

name		our		wish
came		out		dish
game		about		fish
	same	you	your	

ink		eat		take
drink		sea		cake
milk		read		make
	rich	much	made	

God		far		put
soft		car		pull
from		cart		full
	doll	clean	part	

D6

hand		jam		long
sand		jar		song
land		jump		for
	are	morning	stand	

nest		ship		say
best		slip		day
rest		skip		today
	saw	help	play	

44

age	ride	deep
cage	side	keep
page	hide	sleep

time feet into

D7

bite	may	ever
white	way	every
like	away	never

stay mile very

coat	went	ice
boat	sent	nice
road	bent	drop

with sell bend

head	mine	room
bread	line	moon
lost	nine	soon

school have five

D8

pay	rope	cup
bay	hope	pup
hay	hole	under

pole lay said

pipe	feed	now
wipe	need	cow
ripe	sheep	how

were paper down

boy		gave			round
toy		give			ground
flag		live			found
	count	hall	mouth		

rain		find			home
train		kind			nose
again		wind			rose
	going	doing	raining		

D9

other		father			ate
mother		winter			late
brother		summer			gate
	sister	able	table		

dinner		back			fly
supper		black			dry
butter		sick			seven
	water	bill	duck		

snow		kitten			sorry
blow		letter			funny
grow		lesson			sunny
	little	show	happy		

arm		girl			one
hard		bird			love
dark		first			come
	coming	making	river		

D10

spoke	hair	pretty
smoke	chair	dress
fire	fair	grass

baby story fairy

fast	sold	penny
last	cold	add
each	colder	apple

over only after

ear	talk	house
hear	walk	mouse
dear	horse	than

year near ask

face	eye	more
race	eyes	store
left	tail	plant

wait miss lady

GROUP 2

D11

lamp	rent	wing
camp	spent	swing
damp	spend	sting

stamp   string   west

spin	rock	lump
skin	lock	pump
plan	clock	blunt

block   stick   plum

seed	hang	pick
weed	sang	brick
bleed	rang	trick

seem   pack   crack

pond	rush	band
fond	brush	bank
chop	crush	thank

just   shot   chin

D12

cave	shell	drive
wave	smell	drive
save	swell	driver

brave   crane   safe

hood	club	lake
stood	hunt	bake
hook	hunter	baker
	rise sake spoon	

meet	rake	lift
street	wake	list
sheet	awake	mist
	week three named	

date	bee	fine
hate	free	shine
plate	queen	pine
	mate case chase	

D13

creep	chain	pile
sleep	pain	smile
asleep	paint	while
	sleeping painting waiting	

cost	wide	lace
frost	slide	place
frog	life	grand
	wife son grandfather	

push	myself	moth
bush	herself	hoped
stem	himself	kiss
	itself neck body	

49

fold	mind		snap
scold	wild		strap
held	child		both
	blind	children	another

D14

lick	horn		crab
kick	born		swim
thick	gas		storm
	quick	joy	ticket

park	tea		most
bark	teach		post
mark	teacher		stamp
	market	corn	corner

poor	roof		yard
door	window		card
floor	broom		garden
	bedroom	shade	spade

barn	less		meat
harm	bless		heat
farm	press		beat
	neat	such	farmer

D15

fear	pass		town
clear	class		brown
heard	glass		flower
	belt	leaf	bunch

pink	east	sail
think	feast	pail
flat	beast	nail

fail   mix   least

lame	drill	cream
blame	spill	dream
tame	spell	meal

spelling   shame   suck

die	pool	turn
pie	cool	burn
lie	food	hurt

lies   church   curl

D16

oak	ready	sir
goat	dead	dirt
load	death	firm

shirt   third   died

air	night	word
pair	right	world
stair	bright	forget

upstairs   downstairs   tonight

inside	low	star
outside	slow	start
within	crow	sharp

without   own   throw

bow		walking		walked
row		talking		talked
follow		thinking		asked
	looked	looking	maid	

D17

who		nor		speak
which		doctor		speaking
why		fork		reading
	pork	trip	whip	

opening		alive		loud
opened		along		cloud
washed		became		hour
	north	south	filled	

playground		master		babies
football		basket		ladies
march		tiny		stories
	new	party	dance	

having		tooth		seen
giving		teeth		green
living		bath		feel
	riding	heel	once	

D18

cherry		jelly		carry
cherries		jolly		carried
berries		tomorrow		shall
	berry	merry	marry	

rice		paw		bean
mice		raw		lean
pence		draw		mean
	lead	beads	gay	
crying		flies		beach
cried		cries		reach
tried		tries		easy
	warm	please	great	
skipping		stopped		bigger
dropping		dropped		biggest
running		getting		better
	their	two	slippers	

D19

before		any		fresh
below		many		felt
belong		anything		melt
	nothing	beside	behind	
oil		few		know
boil		dew		knew
join		drew		grew
	blew	off	point	
pound		kept		use
sound		desk		used
bound		key		puppy
	even	ox	oxen	

D20

sale	learn	would
tale	early	could
later	strong	cross

these   those   thin

number	note	played
ruler	woke	stayed
uncle	stone	clever

drove   whole   next

done	does	true
gone	goes	blue
bone	inch	silk

some   longer   longest

GROUP 3

D21

team	slave	front
steam	shave	month
scream	grave	Monday
gleam	cape	ton
shape	treat won	wonder

paying	upper	rode
playing	sudden	globe
saying	suffer	joke
staying	offer	poker
pray	plays flutter	close

vain	thunder	soil
plain	peal	spoil
obtain	stuck	noise
faint	struck	swift
shock burst	moment	rainbow

pocket	needle	light
silver	button	sight
money	sew	might
honey	print	fight
stockings	high sigh	fright

D22

robber	real	proud
ladder	deal	pride
bottom	steal	spite
rabbit	leap	rage

bear   wear   tear   pear

singing	begin	prince
bringing	began	princess
blowing	begun	crown
feeling	music	crowd

lord   state   gain   main

sow	turnip	vine
grain	straw	wine
wheat	claw	grape
pea	drawing	field

depart   travel   return   remain

animal	port	prison
donkey	tide	pardon
monkey	shore	forgive
monkeys	coast	punish

lion   rude   swan   polite

D23

gather	owl	arrow
rather	growl	narrow
path	chicken	sorrow
enter	crust	borrow

yellow   pillow   understand   understood

shallow	anger	pale
stream	hunger	shake
moss	hungry	snake
carpet	drank	danger

wade trade sash splash

March	form	large
April	thorn	charge
May	marble	strange
trust	tumble	stranger

someone something sometimes stable

sort	Sunday	dusty
sport	Thursday	stormy
handle	Friday	frosty
candle	unless	cloudy

anybody nobody happen cannot

D24

lamb	sleepy	stove
comb	dirty	glove
crumb	busy	cover
thumb	lucky	shelter

climb steady none become

brain	power	roll
brow	shower	rolled
chest	tower	rolling
cheek	towel	pulled

heart act cottage pudding

match	June	picking
catch	July	picked
patch	September	learned
watch	November	reached

fetch   ditch   snatch   everyone

care	infant	tender
careless	darling	gentle
useless	cradle	weak
useful	young	dull

purse   nurse   fur   beak

D25

hammer	too	lunch
bench	tool	buy
blade	stool	beef
wire	fool	cloth

blood   goose   geese   cheese

change	break	brighter
changed	broke	brightest
taken	broken	safer
eaten	stole	safest

cooler   deeper   finer   miner

hiding	skate	chief
shining	skating	thief
smiling	darkness	grief
hoping	illness	burnt

should   cheer   quickly   nearly

D26

write	prove	grey
writing	move	clay
wrote	remove	poem
wrap	repeat	poet

remark   repair   Easter   Christmas

aloud	coal	yesterday
around	roast	afternoon
alike	cloak	however
afraid	float	breakfast

roam   grandmother   above   usual

branch	classes	together
branches	glasses	towards
peach	order	afterwards
peaches	border	forward

inches   worth   starve   husband

D27

price	pepper	visit
twice	copper	fir
since	cuff	birth
fence	stuff	birthday

bitter   silly   stiff   hurry

provide	dwell	friend
pretend	present	quiet
forest	lemon	boxes
track	sugar	dishes

finger   flesh   wool   bloom

cling	serve	four
strip	person	fourth
pint	term	fifth
gift	upset	tenth

eleven   simple   twelve   hundred

D28

daisy	wise	earn
daisies	spider	earth
lily	soap	grace
lilies	soak	space

voice   bravely   invite   chance

steep	thirteen	thirty
steel	fourteen	twenty
wheel	fifteen	fifty
deed	sixteen	sixty

thousand   creeping   indeed   between

half	halves	flew
calf	leaves	threw
shelf	thieves	crew
loaf	loaves	chew

wolf   themselves   grind   thrown

D29

knee	knife	mail
kneel	knives	rail
knot	wives	snail
knock	fixed	jail

flock   finish   tie   tied

raise	cure	capture
raised	sure	defend
trunk	pure	dying
strike	picture	lying
dread	deaf heaven	paid

built	battle	kettle
build	rattle	bottle
building	cattle	cork
content	tired	sore
rate	flame frame	scrape

D30

swimming	toe	trying
slipped	scout	flying
matter	shout	army
manner	axe	rank
shy spy	butterfly	answer

heavy	easier	cause
heavier	easiest	because
heaviest	easily	instant
war	merrily	shadow
arch	starch touch	being

past	copy	taste
mast	pity	waste
fasten	empty	haste
odd	plenty	good-bye
loss	lose glory	history

GROUP 4

D31

manage	remind	slice
savage	respond	spice
package	repent	notice
postage	record	police

report import export forty

proper	damage	silent
property	voyage	parent
consist	advantage	absent
conduct	wages	serpent

prevent silence remarkable blanket

purple	former	also
furnish	organ	almost
curtain	orchard	already
Saturday	coward	always

murder altogether although comfort

harvest	perhaps	pitch
garment	permit	stitch
alarm	perfect	kitchen
farther	sermon	stretch

cargo artist enjoy enjoyed

D32

tease	oven	linen
weave	woven	often
preach	golden	hasten
beneath	dozen	listen

cheap　　seam　eagle　eager

hotel	armour	intend
camel	parlour	inspect
label	colour	interest
angel	favour	kingdom

favourite　bacon　apron　grasp

castle	grown	fare
thistle	blown	bare
whistle	widow	dare
whisper	velvet	stare

human　woman　women　spare

stain	explain	idle
contain	expect	island
captain	express	share
Britain	extent	pantry

fountain　mountain　certain　extra

D33

paddle	playmate	hoof
meddle	newspaper	smooth
middle	platform	stoop
cripple	fortnight	stooped

settle　midday　midnight　choose

draper	county	limit
grate	country	spirit
scale	cousin	timid
escape	message	public

Wales   Scotland   England   English

laugh	lately	motor
laughed	safely	visitor
laughter	nicely	victory
linger	lovely	inform

lonely   likely   likeness   weakness

servant	though	arrive
merchant	through	advice
distant	empire	adventure
important	admire	nature

constant   admit   amuse   ashamed

D34

evening	object	sailor
event	subject	tailor
equator	robin	railway
enough	holiday	daily

rough   tough   rainy   rocky

sparrow	village	ought
swallow	cabbage	bought
valley	carrot	brought
valleys	gallop	fought

thought   ragged   scatter   brass

alone	nasty	vanish
across	hasty	banish
among	shady	perish
against	study	parish

fancy ugly polish Welsh

lawn	lays	beauty
dawn	laying	beautiful
famous	laid	careful
dangerous	thankful	carefully

faithfully welcome until unable

D35

glance	protect	stumble
advance	monster	grumble
distance	bough	thimble
France	plough	tremble

scramble bundle kindle noble

tight	bucket	error
slight	trumpet	terror
delight	shrub	ribbon
mighty	liberty	cotton

Scottish mutton blossom correct

chalk	gaze	discover
stalk	blaze	distinct
salt	razor	discuss
alter	lazy	distress

size prize dislike disgrace

nation	company	rubber
station	companion	bullet
dictation	astonish	quarrel
motion	publish	barrel

question   appear   quart   quarter

D36

horrid	belief	wharf
coffee	believe	wharves
occur	grieve	niece
occurred	ourselves	piece

occupy   hollow   forgotten   combine

caught	stir	knit
taught	stirred	knitting
daughter	mirror	knight
naughty	bonnet	skill

office   officer   different   skirt

potato	value	instead
potatoes	continue	steadily
tomato	statue	weary
tomatoes	thread	wearily

foe   poetry   butcher   shilling

tunnel	pleasant	groan
suppose	pleasure	coach
cunning	measure	toast
muddy	treasure	throat

defeat   tiger   reward   shoe

D37

obey	dwelling	group
obeyed	wedding	wound
swept	herring	youth
crept	vessel	calm

prettier   prettiest   beginning   journey

recall	demand	feather
result	deliver	leather
beyond	depend	weather
shiver	delay	breath

health   healthy   wealthy   meant

fleet	drown	aim
screen	drowned	claim
greedy	powder	praise
freedom	petrol	dairy

deer   steer   queer   engage

D38

guilty	season	medal
guide	reason	metal
guest	crimson	mental
warn	iron	board

Briton   British   Irish   Ireland

relate	desire	bathe
retire	deserve	vase
restore	behave	rare
refuse	bravery	square

December   October   Germany   herd

attend	edge	flour
attack	hedge	sour
wreck	badge	trout
wrong	judge	stout

lodge   bridge   sword   check

D39

suit	member	wore
fruit	remember	score
orange	remembered	whom
banana	memory	whether

bowl   factory   basement   pavement

using	eight	figure
during	weight	scripture
duty	weigh	creature
truth	dumb	entertain

pour   court   shoulder   huge

exchange	reply	worship
except	drying	worse
excuse	carrying	worst
piano	foggy	worry

city   cities   circle   palace

D40

giant	coin	earnest
engine	noisy	search
divide	sign	French
mistake	signal	honest

seldom   quite   wicked   selfish

throne	area	local
choke	idea	several
clothes	family	second
owe	people	fortune

cruel   Tuesday   Wednesday   disgust

picnic	aunt	pencil
arithmetic	saucer	ocean
flood	farewell	collar
wooden	else	clumsy

holy   pony   navy   losing

GROUP 5

D41

address	regret	lawyer
afford	regard	gardener
assist	retreat	passenger
approach	respect	drawer
account	nerve	chapter

apply   allow   allowed   clown   refer

direct	ankle	confess
detect	sparkle	confine
destroy	humble	confuse
destroyed	feeble	consider
describe	steeple	convict

vote   devote   vast   plaster   pastime

inhabit	educate	pupil
insist	education	peril
invent	information	profit
industry	position	credit
increase	composition	splendid

stupid   insect   sole   dose   whose

D42

future	dismiss	final
pasture	display	finally
furniture	dismay	gradual
manufacture	disorder	gradually
departure	disappear	usually

failure   total   equal   equally   really

Africa	breeze	wonderful
America	freeze	respectful
Canada	squeeze	awful
Atlantic	sleeve	yawn
Pacific	agreeable	fully

China   Arctic   frozen   degree   gem

hero	pickle	climate
heroes	knuckle	private
negro	trample	cultivate
negroes	title	decorate
echo	entitle	decoration

chorus   single   jungle   article   measles

D43

Europe	mere	fraction
Asia	merely	direction
India	sincere	condition
Australia	sincerely	reduction
Russia	severe	protection

telephone   switch   sketch   lantern   fern

terrible	saddle	northern
horrible	struggle	southern
possible	puzzle	eastern
impossible	latter	western
improve	parrot	shepherd

limb   modern   modest   screw   nephew

double	dispute	regular
trouble	displease	popular
couple	disobey	particular
courage	district	singular
encourage	disturb	vinegar

flourish   prey   victim   cigar   calendar

D44

erect	canal	mistress
elect	capital	misfortune
election	rural	mischief
electric	mortal	handkerchief
halt	funeral	handsome

trial   loyal   royal   rascal   musical

detain	procure	revive
retain	endure	revenge
complain	feature	reverse
bargain	torture	resolve
waist	secure	resemble

secret　select　request　require　inquire

ordinary	image	exact
library	imagine	exactly
January	imagination	expand
February	examine	extract
enemy	examination	exercise

exist　example　bury　buried　ivy

D45

loan	preserve	fortunate
coax	prepare	unfortunate
oath	compare	moderate
active	beware	estimate
action	betray	happiness

compose　advise　promise　glimpse　sense

wrestle	beggar	produce
wrist	cellar	promote
written	pillar	progress
gentlemen	grammar	possess
heathen	burglar	entire

chimney　turkey　tune　tube　costume

discontent	grocer	mention
represent	groceries	attention
evident	tempt	situation
frequent	attempt	invitation
accident	temptation	truly

elbow   growth   speech   graze   naked

D46

accept	honour	labour
according	harbour	devour
plunge	habit	justice
population	pigeon	practice
satin	gulf	service

sober   basin   cabin   rapid   payment

excite	construct	explore
exciting	contribute	exploration
excellent	consume	explanation
exclaim	confirm	style
exclaimed	contrast	pavement

expel   angry   envy   idea   oblige

height	junior	gospel
either	language	compel
neither	monument	chapel
reign	department	jewel
foreign	swear	bushel

parcel   course   veil   vein   neighbour

D47

supply	avenue	government
support	diamond	madam
attract	foundation	passage
arrest	fuel	bandage
shrink	cruelly	separate

enclose terror magic dye ruin

latitude	employ	observe
altitude	employer	observation
minute	custom	desert
reduce	customer	slavery
refuge	fever	misery

violin violet cricket clerk onion

common	errand	arrange
collect	funnel	arranging
connect	flannel	gallery
connection	channel	difficult
command	current	umbrella

neglect prospect suspect villain cannon

D48

argue	citizen	surprise
argument	century	purchase
valuable	centre	purpose
vegetable	central	further
comfortable	hospital	scratch

complete estate minister receive deceive

scare   insane   entrance
scarce   invade   performance
scarf   inspire   balance
meanness   include   substance
straight   introduce   lightning
  dodge   pledge   divine   ache   headache

adopt   guard   decide
prompt   guess   recite
cupboard   guinea   concert
sponge   tongue   fertile
problem   rogue   unite
  mercy   multiply   ninth   fashion   thirsty

D49

uniform   expense   ninety
perform   expensive   safety
force   relative   surely
skull   standard   entirely
utmost   scholar   o'clock
    period   roar   soar   cocoa   situated

general   embrace   threat
generally   surface   weapon
practical   furnace   forehead
natural   wasp   heaviness
naturally   sleepiness   weariness
  annual   cough   ounce   soup   business

---

bicycle	permission	orphan
biscuit	admission	geography
juice	million	elephant
statement	region	abundant
improvement	union	colony

sentence   defence   peace   appeal   instantly

D50

author	August	brief
governor	autumn	priest
conductor	fault	shriek
scent	pause	fierce
scene	laundry	view

scenery   length   depth   submit   subtract

choice	curious	arouse
rejoice	various	trousers
avoid	glorious	surround
moisture	anxious	surrender
palm	worthy	wither

abrupt   lungs   fury   material   special

woollen	carriage	succeed
crooked	marriage	success
loose	machine	successful
foolish	acre	prayer
soldier	pearl	deny

New Zealand   zone   debt   doubt

GROUP 6

D51

personal	declare	portion
liberal	decrease	proportion
festival	decline	production
removal	determine	protection
criminal	determination	introduction

fund   minor   majority   traitor

greet	accurate	insult
Greece	accuse	instruct
engineer	accustom	insert
pioneer	announce	injure
career	addition	injury

keen   ghost   skeleton   cushion   income

contract	prefer	wholesome
control	preferred	enterprise
consent	conferred	therefore
contempt	grudge	wireless
conclude	lodging	grateful

convince   poison   coil   wisdom   condemn

D52

hesitate	continent	stage
delicate	fragment	garage
candidate	regiment	average
certificate	experiment	discourage
navigate	cement	baggage

debate   student   confident   camera   remedy

treaty	lecture	nervous
treatment	agriculture	prosperous
ornament	temperate	tremendous
instrument	temperature	ridiculous
prominent	puncture	jealous

recent   recently   volcano   couch   route

sensible	ignorant	ceiling
responsible	ignorance	perceive
visible	abundance	deceit
invisible	attendance	deceitful
rifle	appearance	earthquake

hatred   sacred   witch   wretched   wrinkle

D53

telescope	national	conversation
telegram	cathedral	consideration
telegraph	principal	sensation
photograh	punctual	combination
physical	continually	ventilation

phrase   fatal   section   intention   choir

domestic	tenant	fragment
athletic	vacant	insurance
heroic	tyrant	assistance
majestic	elegant	remembrance
tropics	extravagant	circumstance

item   ideal   pilot   pistol   seize

miserable	despair	convert
reasonable	despise	concern
capable	description	convey
probable	destruction	witness
probably	energy	cleanliness

liable   reliable   angle   trifle   muscle

D54

influence	famine	reception
presence	medicine	ambition
evidence	genuine	satisfaction
residence	granite	objection
reference	definite	instruction

absence   pretence   umpire   crime   circus

salute	detail	acquire
distribute	deposit	acquaint
gratitude	develop	acquainted
destitute	strength	acquaintance
volume	strengthen	disappoint

luxury   burden   swollen   execute   abbey

pattern	release	offend
messenger	reveal	oppose
traveller	reflect	opposite
challenge	reserve	opposition
college	remainder	application

response   resign   design   oppress   approve

D55

flavour	generous	innocent
vapour	numerous	independent
rumour	enormous	excitement
occasion	mischievous	advertise
occasionally	marvellous	advertisement

practise   impudent   yield   shield   pierce

invalid	digest	provoke
invention	digestion	proclaim
patient	soul	pronounce
impatient	mould	proceed
impatience	poultry	opinion

frigid   civil   civilized   operation   heir

commit	comrade	pension
commence	complaint	provision
recommend	humour	decision
recollect	endeavour	conclusion
shipping	tobacco	division

solve   dissolve   wholly   annoy   annoyed

D56

poverty	margin	transform
mutiny	origin	translate
variety	original	character
society	moral	programme
sacrifice	crystal	sandwich

arrival   Spain   dainty   quaint   quench

create suitable Chinese
creation creditable interfere
emigrate honourable supreme
emigrant peaceable extreme
obstinate manageable extremely
scheme pursue pursuit mourn source

intelligent judgment thorough
intelligence parliament sustain
difference incident maintain
offence magnificent portrait
apparent compliment quarry
torrent squirrel essay type typewriter

D57

vulgar boundary convenient
similar tributary convenience
irregular missionary experience
circular salary obedient
military extraordinary obedience
existence consequence psalm attach fowl

ascend plague obstacle
descend league miracle
science fatigue spectacle
scissors disguise violent
intimate disaster permanent
rear breathe cease conceal awkward

university	social	precious
opportunity	artificial	gracious
possibility	especially	delicious
responsibility	musician	suspicious
curiosity	triumph	suspicion

charity   ability   brooch   stomach   wreath

D58

religion	necessary	exceed
religious	necessity	exclude
previous	furious	exception
victorious	serious	expedition
industrious	behaviour	explode

solemn   prophet   scarlet   excursion   saviour

distinguish	system	persevere
extinguish	sympathy	atmosphere
persuade	mystery	electricity
establish	delivery	interrupt
diminish	discovery	settler

abolish   leisure   sovereign   urge   urgent

pressure	affection	scribble
assure	affectionate	ruffle
assume	attraction	rubbish
assent	accomplish	summit
assemble	accompany	traffic

appoint   affair   twilight   coarse   hoarse

D59

nursery	organize	occupation
jewellery	organization	congregation
machinery	realize	preparation
prospect	recognize	separation
satisfy	horizon	champion

collection   attractive   novel   marvel   cancel

celebrate	passion	interior
celebration	impression	exterior
illustrate	discussion	inferior
chocolate	possession	superior
immediately	correspond	senior

imitate   imitation   soothe   indulge   indulging

benefit	audience	exhaust
benefited	authority	exhibit
profited	clause	exhibition
partner	applaud	register
privilege	cautious	nourish

launch   breadth   suburb   council   album

D60

nonsense	knowledge	instructor
suspense	acknowledge	conquer
condense	postpone	conqueror
immense	envelope	radiator
intense	liquid	mayor

dense   haughty   slaughter   curve   disease

peculiar	associate	scorch
familiar	association	horror
brilliant	appreciation	stubborn
Spaniard	official	Christian
Spanish	sufficient	positive

ancient	hymn	column	bruise	survive

courteous	rescue	skilful
courageous	virtue	pitiful
museum	issue	welfare
unusual	procession	fulfil
suggest	succession	ceremony

siege	salmon	Egypt	absurd	theatre

Supplementary Spelling List of New Words

These are words which were not in Schonell's original Essential Spelling List. This supplementary list has been added to this edition to assist teachers in selecting and teaching those new words which children need and use today. See Introduction to New Edition pp. 3–4 for further explanation.

GROUP 2

video	robot	comic
stereo	riot	plastic
bingo	slot	elastic

snooker	cartoon	balloon

GROUP 3

cheque	shuttle	jeans
antique	battery	anorak
mosque	lottery	sweater
plaque	cassette	trainers

metric litre gram metre

GROUP 4

centimetre	aerial	fridge
millimetre	racial	freezer
kilometre	rental	vacuum
kilogram	digital	radio

millilitre terminal thermal television

Pakistan	missile	quartz
Zimbabwe	mission	qualify
Israel	dissolve	quiz
Poland	tissue	quilt

Hindu Muslim Jew Sikh

GROUP 5

hovercraft	nylon	microwave
helicopter	pylon	microphone
submarine	neon	microscope
aeroplane	silicon	microchip
caravan	marathon	microfilm

detector calculator escalator obsolete concrete

computer	communist	mechanic
computerized	socialist	static
data	fascist	ethnic
program	racist	acrylic
function	tourist	electronic

supersonic synthetic terrorist catalogue analogue

GROUP 6

insulation	universe	disabled
conservation	universal	disposable
radiation	satellite	discotheque
pollution	solar	disconnect
petition	lunar	discount

international polythene polyester
polystyrene distributor

technical	precinct	nuclear
technology	president	reactor
technique	prejudice	uranium
detergent	preservative	plutonium
detective	prescription	atomic

polytechnic comprehensive automatic
autograph astronaut

86

THE NEW GRADED DICTATIONS

The following Dictations review the words given in the Essential Spelling List. Each Dictation refers back to the appropriate number on pp. 42–84 (e.g., D1, D2, D3 etc.) and reviews three or four sets of words.

GROUP 1

1   The man ran in the sun. He is so hot he has to get to the well. He had to run and run. He fell by the well. The man is glad to get wet. (*35 words*)

2.   A man ran up to me in the fog. I had to run. I did not stop. I ran to the shop that is at the top of the hill. It was open. I ran in and hid. (*38 words*)

3.   The king met the men at the mill. He had a good look at all of them. He had to send ten of them into the wood to set the trap. (*31 words*)

4.   The old man had his drum in a box. He sat on this and hid by the tall tree. She had been calling him but he did not want to see her. (*32 words*)

5.   Our car is not the same as your car. My dad made it. He put our name in gold on the boot. It is clean and will take us as far as we wish to go. (*36 words*)

6.   I was about to play on the sand when I saw a ship call for help. I saw the men jump from the side of the ship into the deep sea. It took a long time for help to get to them. (*42 words*)

7. We had a <u>bite</u> of <u>bread</u> and then <u>went</u> into the <u>boat</u>. It was <u>very</u> small. There was <u>room</u> for <u>five</u> of us, but <u>nine</u> had to go by <u>road</u>. We had a long <u>way</u> to go and I was <u>soon</u> glad that I had my <u>coat</u> <u>with</u> me. (*49 words*)

8   It was <u>raining</u> and the <u>boy</u> was very wet but he had to <u>find</u> the lost <u>sheep</u>. He <u>found</u> it. The sheep was in a deep <u>hole</u>. <u>How</u> was he <u>going</u> to get it out? The boy <u>lay</u> <u>down</u> on the <u>ground</u>. He put a <u>rope</u> <u>under</u> the sheep. He had to pull <u>again</u> and again. He <u>gave</u> a big tug and the sheep came out. (*66 words*)

9   My <u>sister</u> and I were <u>coming</u> <u>back</u> from the <u>river</u> where we had seen a <u>black</u> <u>duck</u> on the <u>water</u>. We were <u>late</u> for <u>dinner</u> and we had to run. When we got in my <u>brother</u> was at the <u>table</u>. My sister ran in <u>first</u> but she fell. Her <u>arm</u> hit the table. The <u>butter</u> fell into my brother's lap. I found it <u>funny</u> but my <u>mother</u> was not so <u>happy</u>. (*71 words*)

10 On a <u>cold</u> day <u>last</u> <u>year</u> I went for a <u>walk</u> in the wood. I came to a little <u>house</u>. An old <u>lady</u> came out and went <u>over</u> to a <u>horse</u>. She gave him an <u>apple</u>. I <u>spoke</u> but she did not <u>hear</u> me. She had long white <u>hair</u> and a <u>pretty</u> <u>face</u> but her <u>eyes</u> were sad. She went back in and <u>after</u> a time I <u>left</u>. (*68 words*)

GROUP 2

11 Tom did not hear the <u>crack</u>. I <u>just</u> had time to <u>spin</u> round when I saw the <u>lump</u> of <u>rock</u> fall. I had to <u>rush</u> over and push him out of the way. We saw it <u>crush</u> the <u>camp</u> we had <u>spent</u> all day making, but we were glad that it had not hit us. We had to <u>pick</u> up our things and <u>brush</u> the dust from them. We then made our camp again, but this time we went down to the river <u>bank</u>. (*84 words*)

12 It was cold and damp and the road seemed to <u>shine</u> in the <u>mist</u>. The <u>driver</u> left his car and <u>stood</u> under a <u>street</u> lamp. He was <u>safe</u> at last. The <u>three</u> men had <u>chased</u> him for a long way but he had a fast car and in the end he had lost them. He <u>lifted</u> the lid of his <u>case</u> and took out a small black book. This was what the men were after. It was very late but he had to stay <u>awake</u>. It was not over yet. (*90 words*)

13 I saw <u>both</u> the <u>children</u> <u>smile</u> as our <u>grandfather</u> looked for a <u>place</u> to put the <u>painting</u> of <u>himself</u>. He <u>held</u> it up on one wall but

it was too <u>wide</u>. He held it up to <u>another</u> wall but it was still too big. It took a long time but at last he found a place to hang it. He left the room to get his <u>wife</u> but <u>while</u> we were <u>waiting</u> for him to come back there was a loud <u>snap</u> and the painting fell down. (*87 words*)

14 <u>Mark</u> had to be <u>quick</u>. The <u>barn</u> was on fire and all the <u>corn</u> was stored in there. <u>Thick</u> black smoke was coming out of the <u>door</u> and the <u>roof</u> looked as if it was about to cave in. He raced round the <u>corner</u> of the <u>yard</u> and called for help. The <u>farmer</u> looked out of the <u>bedroom</u> <u>window</u> and rushed down. Other men came and they soon <u>beat</u> out the fire but <u>most</u> of the corn had been lost. (*80 words*)

15 The <u>town</u> lived in <u>fear</u> of the <u>beast</u> and they ran into the <u>church</u> if ever they <u>heard</u> it coming. But one day a little girl did not <u>turn</u> and run away. She waited in the road and the beast walked up to her. It did not <u>hurt</u> her. She held out some <u>food</u> on the <u>flat</u> of her hand and the beast ate it. It was <u>tame</u> from that day on. (*72 words*)

16 I will not <u>forget</u> last <u>night</u> for a long time. I went <u>downstairs</u> to get a drink and as I passed one of our rooms I <u>looked</u> in and saw three men. I saw one of them <u>throw</u> a <u>pair</u> of gold cups into a case, I saw another man <u>load</u> up a sack but the <u>third</u> man just stood <u>outside</u>. The men did not say a <u>word</u>. I stood very still but all the time I was <u>thinking</u> about what I must do. <u>Without</u> making a sound I <u>walked</u> back <u>upstairs</u> to get help. (*95 words*)

17 Ben was walking <u>along</u> and <u>reading</u> at the same time. I saw him <u>trip</u> over a <u>basket</u> and step right into a tin of paint <u>which</u> had just been <u>opened</u>. He looked down at his feet. They were <u>green</u>. We called to his mother <u>who</u> came out at <u>once</u> and <u>washed</u> his feet They were still green. He sat in the <u>bath</u> for an <u>hour</u> but they were still green. Ben said he did not mind <u>having</u> green feet so we left them like that. (*85 words*)

18 Pat <u>stopped</u> <u>running</u> along the <u>beach</u> and bent down. She <u>cried</u> out, 'Look, I have found the <u>biggest</u> pair of <u>slippers</u> in the world.' She dug them out of the sand and held them up. The man who had <u>dropped</u> them must have had <u>great</u> big feet. Just for fun we all <u>tried</u> them on. Pat asked, 'Why did someone bring <u>their</u>

slippers here?' They looked new so we <u>carried</u> them back with us and hoped that <u>tomorrow</u> we might find out who owned them. (*85 words*)

19 The <u>key</u> was in my <u>desk</u>. I did not <u>know</u> where it had come from. It did not <u>belong</u> to me and I had never seen it <u>before</u>. I picked it up and as I held the key it <u>grew</u> bigger and bigger. It <u>felt</u> warm and then it jumped off my hand and lay on the floor <u>beside</u> me. <u>Even</u> as I looked it seemed to <u>melt</u> away and after a while there was <u>nothing</u> left. I <u>knew</u> I must never say <u>anything</u> about what I had seen. (*89 words*)

20 Every summer I <u>stayed</u> with my <u>uncle</u> but I had never been in the room <u>next</u> to mine. <u>Early</u> each morning he <u>drove</u> into town and on my last day I waited until he had <u>gone</u> before I went into the room. It was full of <u>stones</u>. I picked up the <u>longest</u> one I <u>could</u> find. On the top was a <u>cross</u> in <u>thin</u> <u>blue</u> lines. I heard my uncle coming back so I put the stone down and left the room. I never did <u>learn</u> why he had all <u>those</u> stones. (*92 words*)

GROUP 3

21 There were five of us in the lift when it came to a <u>sudden</u> stop last <u>Monday</u>. It had <u>stuck</u> just below one of the <u>upper</u> floors so we were very <u>high</u>. The <u>light</u> went out and a baby <u>screamed</u>. It was a <u>shock</u> and for a <u>moment</u> we all stood still. I was <u>close</u> to the <u>buttons</u> so I felt for them and pushed the last one. A bell rang and before long I could hear a <u>faint</u> <u>noise</u> outside and then the lift started going again. We had all had a bit of a <u>fright</u> but we were safe now. (*102 words*)

22 Ben was <u>feeling</u> very <u>proud</u> of his new hat. It was blue with red spots and made of <u>real</u> wool. He had saved for months to get the hat and now at last he was able to <u>wear</u> it, but as he walked home a strong wind was <u>blowing</u> and the hat blew right off his head. Ben saw it flutter down on to the top of a tree. He ran home and <u>returned</u> with a <u>ladder</u>. He put this at the <u>bottom</u> of the tree and went up. Ben got his hat back without any <u>tears</u> in it. (*99 words*)

23 Martin was woken up by a <u>strange</u> <u>sort</u> of clicking noise. <u>Something</u> or <u>someone</u> was in his room. He put on the light and his eyes went wide with fear. Moving over his <u>carpet</u> was a <u>large</u>

yellow snake. Martin went pale and began to shake. He was in
real danger. He could not understand where it had come from or
even how it had entered the room, but now he had to do
something about it and there was nobody to help him. He threw
his pillow over the snake and charged out of the room. (*97
words*)

24 When I found the young bird in the ditch he was not much bigger
than my thumb. He had hurt his wing and was very weak. I
fetched an old lady that I knew. She reached down and with great
care she picked up the tiny animal and cradled him in her hands.
She was so gentle. Each day I watched her nurse him and put
crumbs of food into his beak. By the end of July he was better
and we had to let him go. I felt the tears rolling down my cheeks
as I watched him fly away. (*101 words*)

25 The miners had just eaten lunch when there was a crashing sound
and rocks started falling from the roof. The men ran deeper into
the mine. They were now in darkness and rocks blocked their
way out. One man said it would be safer if they stayed still and
saved air by not talking too much. Each man was hoping that
help would come quickly. After many hours they heard the
sound of men with hammers trying to break up the rocks. They
could see a faint light shining and it was getting brighter all the
time. They knew that help had nearly reached them. (*105
words*)

26 My grandmother cannot see very well without her glasses.
However, yesterday afternoon I found her trying to write
without them. She told me that she had lost them. She said that
after breakfast she had changed the sheets and then, in order to
comb her hair, she had removed her glasses. Together we looked
around every room but I began to feel afraid that we would never
find them. I went back into the bedroom and this time I saw a
lump in the bed. I moved forward and pulled back the covers and
there were her glasses. (*98 words*)

27 I shall never forget my tenth birthday last November. My friend
came to visit and we went to play by the flats. We were digging a
hole by the fence when I saw something shining in the mud. We
dug deeper and found four copper boxes. Our fingers were stiff
with cold but we pulled out the boxes and opened their lids. We

both went quiet. Each box held twelve silver coins that were twice as big as any I had ever seen. They might have been there for hundreds of years and they were the best present I had that birthday. (102 words)

28 It was dark and Jane stopped to look at her watch. It was eleven thirty. At that moment something jumped in front of her. It was more like a spider than a man and it began to grind something up between its fingers. It then threw the dust over Jane and she could understand what it was saying. In a gentle voice it said that twenty of them had come to Earth from another world in space. It invited her back to meet the crew but she was afraid to take the chance. Half an hour later Jane watched as something large flew into the night sky. (*107 words*)

29 The old man had to kneel down to open the box. Inside it was the picture of a building. It had been his home for fifty years and now they were going to knock it down and build on the land. He walked down to see his old house, but it had gone. There were piles of bricks and the window frames were being burned. He went closer. Lying on the ground was a knife that he had lost years ago. He scraped off the mud and held it in his hand. He felt tired. He watched the flames for a while and then walked away. (*106 words*)

30 The spy broke the lock and slipped easily into the building. He had plenty to do and could not waste any time. It was much easier than he could have hoped for because the place seemed to be empty. He quickly found the right room but now he had to find the file so he could make a copy of the writing. While he was trying to open the desk he heard someone shout and the shadow of a man went past the door. Before he left he made sure that nobody would know that anything had been touched. (*99 words*)

GROUP 4

31 Colin went to the house on Saturday. The property had been empty for almost twenty years, ever since the murder. His parents were always telling him that no one had wanted to live there after the man had been taken by the police. Colin noticed that the wood over the windows was damaged and so he

managed to climb inside. It was pitch dark and silent. He made his way to the kitchen, but the house gave him a strange feeling, and although he was not a coward he knew he should not be there. He left and never went back. (*101 words*)

32 Jill was eager to listen to the record by her favourite group. She played it a dozen times before she turned it over. She was not interested in the other side and did not expect it to be much good. At first there was a whistle and then the whisper of a woman's voice. Jill was certain she could hear her own name being said. She inspected the label but it just gave the name of a song. She put the record on again but this time there was singing. Jill was never able to explain what she had heard. (*100 words*)

33 Every year Ted left England to spend a fortnight in Wales. He always stayed in hotels but this year his spirit of adventure got the better of him. He wanted to be close to nature in that lovely country, and so he intended to go camping. He arrived at midnight and pitched his tent in the middle of a field. He was ashamed to admit that he was a bit lonely but he soon settled safely to sleep. He woke up early and saw a large hoof poking through the edge of his tent. He ran. He wanted to be close to nature, but not that close. (*107 words*)

34 Robin was a good sailor and he had set himself the dangerous job of sailing alone around the world, but now he was in the middle of a bad storm. The sea was so rough that the waves were crashing against his boat and he was almost unable to stand. He thought he had brought enough food and water but they were running out and he had to be careful not to drink too much each day. At dawn on the third day of the storm he was thankful to see a ship coming towards him, it was the most welcome sight he had ever seen. (*106 words*)

35 I was having my lunch on a park bench in France when a crowd of people ran past me shouting. I did not understand them so I carried on eating. I looked up and was astonished to see that an ugly monster had appeared in the distance. It was about twice the size of a man and heading my way. I took one glance and knew I must protect myself. I stumbled to a tree, then scrambled up and held on tight to a bough. I trembled with terror as it picked up my lunch and ate it. I later discovered that it had escaped from the zoo. (*108 words*)

36 The old woman looked in the <u>mirror</u> and made sure that her <u>skirt</u> was clean, she then went downstairs and tried to <u>occupy</u> herself with her <u>knitting</u> while she waited for her <u>daughter</u> to come. It was not <u>often</u> that she had visitors but it gave her so much <u>pleasure</u> when someone did come to visit. She had bought some <u>coffee</u> and had enough <u>pieces</u> of bread to make some <u>toast</u>. She <u>continued</u> to <u>knit</u> <u>steadily</u> but the time went on. The old woman could not <u>believe</u> that her daughter had <u>forgotten</u>, <u>instead</u> she could only <u>suppose</u> that something had delayed her. (*102 words*)

37 Jack Robins was a <u>wealthy</u> man who drove a large car with real <u>leather</u> seats. He always <u>demanded</u> that everyone <u>obey</u> him, he even had his car polished twice a week. Last month he went on a <u>journey</u> to a <u>wedding</u> but when he was just <u>beyond</u> half way his car came to a sudden stop. He <u>wound</u> down the window and called to a <u>group</u> of boys but they were too far away. The <u>weather</u> was so cold he could see his <u>breath</u> and it was <u>beginning</u> to snow. He was too angry about the <u>delay</u> to notice that he had simply run out of <u>petrol</u>. (*107 words*)

38 In <u>December</u> a ship from <u>Germany</u> was <u>wrecked</u> off the coast of <u>Ireland</u>. I was a <u>guest</u> at my cousins at the time and when we heard the alarm we knew the <u>reason</u> and ran to the <u>edge</u> of the beach. I could see that the <u>metal</u> hull had been torn open as the ship had become <u>lodged</u> in the rocks. The men on <u>board</u> were trying to escape but they were being swept over by the crashing waves. One man on the beach <u>refused</u> to be stopped from swimming out to the wreck with some rope. As he dived into the rough sea my cousin said that he <u>deserved</u> a <u>medal</u> for such <u>bravery</u>. (*115 words*)

39 I have a clear <u>memory</u> of that day. <u>During</u> the afternoon I came across a <u>piano</u> on the pavement and <u>eight</u> men were standing in a <u>circle</u> discussing how it could be moved into the <u>basement</u>. I <u>remember</u> thinking that it <u>weighed</u> too much and was the wrong shape to go down the stairs. They were about to give up when a strange <u>figure</u> came out of a nearby <u>factory</u>. He put down the <u>huge</u> sack he was <u>carrying</u> on his <u>shoulder</u> and went over to the piano. He lifted it up and carried it down the steps. Everyone spoke to him afterwards but he did not <u>reply</u>, he picked up his sack and walked away. (*116 words*)

40 For several years my aunt had owned a little French car. She is a
good driver but has no idea how a car works. Last Tuesday she
was supposed to be taking my family to a local picnic area. We
were all ready and waiting when she rang up to say that
something had fallen off her engine and now it seemed to be very
noisy. She told us that the people next door had helped her
search for quite a long time but nobody could find the missing
piece so she would just come with the car as it was. We all knew
the second she had arrived because her car sounded like a
tractor. *(116 words)*

GROUP 5

41 The young policeman held his position behind the wall because
he had a direct view into the house. He had been sent to the
address after being told that a man with a gun was holding a
family. People had described the gunman and the police now had
enough information to know that he was an escaped convict.
They closed off the street and nobody was allowed to enter. The
man in charge considered the problem and knew it would be
stupid to approach the building. He increased the number of
men in the area and waited. He could only hope that the gunman
would lose his nerve and give himself up. *(112 words)*

42 Norman had always been a total failure. Usually, everything he
did went wrong but now he had finally done something right. He
had made a model of the American White House out of sugar
cubes, every single cube had been carefully placed in position
and gradually the building had taken shape. He was really proud
of himself and thought it was wonderful when he was invited to
display his work in America.
      He decided to make the journey by sea but he went on an awful
old ship which sank during a storm. Everyone was rescued but to
his great dismay Norman had to watch as his work of art melted
and then disappeared into the Atlantic Ocean. *(118 words)*

43 The couple had visited so many places, in such a short time, that
it was impossible for them to remember even a fraction of what
they had seen. They struggled to work out in which direction
they were now going, but they were fairly certain that they were
heading for Europe. So far they had been to Australia, China
and Asia, where they had liked India in particular. The man
reminded his wife that they had to telephone his nephew when

they reached England. He then leaned back and rested. She stared out at the carpet of clouds and puzzled over where they had been when her husband had sat on the horrible insect. (*114 words*)

44 The advert for the electric exercise machine claimed that no effort was required from the user but it would revive the whole body in minutes. It was a real bargain so I sent off my money and requested that the machine should be sent as soon as possible.

When it arrived I examined the contents and erected it ready for my trial run. I was not at all disturbed that it closely resembled a means of torture. I secured the leather strap around my waist and, since it was my first time, I selected the slowest speed. What happened then is beyond imagination, but the doctor says that my limbs should stop shaking in about a week. (*117 words*)

45 The beggar had held Jenny's wrist and made her promise never to mention the letter to anyone. He had told her that what was written was important for the entire world, but that it must not be opened for fifty years, no matter how tempted she felt.

Jenny now sat with the letter that she had preserved for exactly fifty years and was finally able to read. She remembered meeting the tramp in a cellar during the war, she remembered his strange speech and she remembered saying that she would not betray his trust.

He had advised her to pay close attention to everything in the letter and as she read on it soon became evident that he had been no ordinary man. (*123 words*)

46 David and Karen had thought it would be exciting to explore the city. However, by midday they were tired and lost. Beside them was a tall monument which, according to the map, did not exist. They stopped one man in the hope that he could put them on course but he spoke in a rapid foreign language which neither of them understood. Karen then had the excellent idea that they should go to the top of the monument because the height would enable them to see their position.

When they reached the top David tripped and dropped his bag. He watched his parcel of cheese sandwiches plunge towards the pavement. He was angry, because now he had lost his way and his lunch. (*123 words*)

47   The pilot was employed by an oil company to collect men and goods and transport them to difficult areas. He had flown over the desert many times but the idea of having to land there still filled him with terror. On this flight he was carrying a member of the government who wanted to observe the oil fields.

They were crossing the desert when the plane began to lose altitude. There was something wrong with the fuel supply. The pilot reduced speed and commanded everyone to prepare for a crash-landing. The next few minutes were terrible, but they managed to use the radio and arrange for help. Nobody was hurt in the crash but the pilot now knew the real misery of his secret fear. (*125 words*)

48   It was the summer fair and Martin was balanced on a box with his head poking through a hole in the centre of a large board. The purpose for this strange position was to allow people to throw wet sponges in his face. Martin decided that he must have been insane to let this happen to him, he even felt a bit scared.

The first customer was a small girl who stuck out her tongue as she took aim. The sponge went straight for Martin but, to everyone's complete surprise, it missed. She threw a further nine sponges and although Martin dodged eight of them the ninth one hit him on the nose. He decided that next year he would run the lucky dip. (*124 words*)

49   The soup factory which is situated at the top of our road has manufactured millions of tins of soup over a period of about ninety years. Until last week's accident.

Nobody is really sure what happened but it is generally believed that a huge storage tank cracked open and the soup instantly rushed out with such force that nothing could stop it. The factory floor was entirely flooded with vegetable soup that had lumps of potato floating on the surface.

At four o'clock the workers were given permission to go home early and the firemen got down to the business of pumping out the building. By the time they had finished, even their uniforms were covered in vegetable soup. (*119 words*)

50   Mr Adams was surrounded by paper as he sat at his desk. A woman entered the study, she walked the length of the room and waited by the window. Mr Adams stood up and in the belt of his trousers was a pearl handled dagger which he removed as he

went towards her. She did not seem <u>anxious</u>, even when he came to an <u>abrupt</u> stop in front of her, but she <u>shrieked</u> as he raised the dagger and then brought his arm down quickly.

After a <u>brief pause</u> he went back to his desk and the woman left the room. He was a <u>successful author</u> of murder stories and he liked to act out <u>various special scenes</u> before he wrote them down. (*123 words*)

GROUP 6

51 The <u>engineer</u> listened as the group of people talked about the <u>condemned</u> house. The <u>majority</u> of them were <u>convinced</u> that the place was haunted and <u>declared</u> that nothing would make them spend a night there. The engineer laughed and everyone looked at him. He <u>announced</u> that there were no such things as <u>ghosts</u> and <u>concluded</u> by saying that he was <u>determined</u> to prove his point by sleeping there alone. Another man was <u>keen</u> to go with him but the engineer said that he <u>preferred</u> to go by himself.

The next night the engineer entered the house with only a blanket and a <u>cushion</u>. He slept soundly, so soundly that he did not see the glowing <u>skeleton</u> as it floated around the room. (*122 words*)

52 A group of <u>students</u> had <u>recently</u> carried out some <u>experiments</u> on the land surrounding a small town in Greece. They had used <u>delicate instruments</u> to measure the <u>temperature</u> and movements of the ground and their results showed that a major <u>earthquake</u> was likely to occur very soon. Six months later their results proved to be accurate.

The ground gave a <u>tremendous</u> shudder, as if the whole <u>continent</u> was splitting open. Everyone ran out of the buildings as <u>ornaments</u> smashed and <u>ceilings</u> fell. Then it was over. Some people gave first aid <u>treatment</u> to the injured while others stared at the <u>fragments</u> that had been their homes. It seemed <u>ridiculous</u> that a tiny movement of the ground could be <u>responsible</u> for all that terrible damage. (*124 words*)

53 The <u>photographs</u> caused a <u>national sensation</u>. They clearly showed a giant space ship from another planet, and the paper said that since the pictures had come from a <u>reliable</u> person it was <u>reasonable</u> to think they were not fakes. Everyone was <u>seized</u> by a sense of <u>despair</u> and excitement.

Many people claimed to have witnessed the craft and they gladly gave descriptions of it. The subject came up in most conversations and one General announced his concern that the craft was capable of the total destruction of the world. Others said that the visitors probably had no intention of hurting us.

A month later a small item appeared in the paper explaining that the pictures had been a combination of dustbin lids and trick photography. (*125 words*)

54 Tony sat in his prison cell and reflected on the pattern of his life. His ambition had been to go to college but his parents had opposed everything he did. They had disapproved of his friends and ideas until he had left home. He went to the city but there was none of the luxury he had imagined and he was soon living among destitutes. He became acquainted with a boy who made his living by stealing. Tony was influenced by him and helped with the crimes, but before long he was caught and there was enough evidence to send him to prison.

Now he just wanted to finish the remainder of his sentence and be released, then he could return home and start again. (*125 words*)

55 My grandmother is a very impatient patient. She recently had a major operation on her hip but refuses to let anyone help her. She loudly proclaims that she is not an invalid and has no intention of being treated like one. On the occasions when we have done something for her she proceeds to tell us that, although she is grateful, she was perfectly capable of doing it herself. She argues that she needs to practise to become wholly independent again, and gets annoyed when we suggest that the doctor would not recommend her to dash about like a lunatic a fortnight after leaving hospital.

We still endeavour to help her, but have reached the conclusion that we must wait until she is not looking. (*125 words*)

56 The main character in the programme was a hero with a difference. *He did not have the magnificent strength of Superman, nor the intelligence of Batman, but he did have the amazing ability to transform himself into a squirrel.

*He did not have the magnificent strength nor the intelligence of other heroes, but he did have... (alternative wording)

It may not seem entirely <u>suitable</u> for a <u>supreme</u> crime fighter to turn into a squirrel but it was an <u>extremely</u> useful way for him to pursue villains without being observed. It also provided him with his most valuable <u>source</u> of information. He could sit in trees and listen to the criminals' conversations and then scramble among the branches to escape from any nasty <u>incidents</u>.

He was very <u>thorough</u> in his attempts to rid <u>society</u> of crime and his only problem was that people kept trying to feed him with bits of their <u>sandwiches</u>. (*133 words*)

57   Danny's mother refused to let him have his hair cut in a <u>similar</u> style to all his friends, so he waited for a suitable <u>opportunity</u> and went into the bathroom with a pair of <u>scissors</u>. He snipped away happily and did not <u>cease</u> until the sink was full of hair, then he stopped and looked carefully at the <u>consequences</u> of his actions. His hair was a disaster. It was quite <u>extraordinary</u> the way it stood up in <u>irregular</u> clumps, in fact it looked as if he was trying to <u>disguise</u> himself as a hedgehog.

He found it very <u>awkward</u> to <u>conceal</u> his hair, <u>especially</u> from his mother, who had her <u>suspicions</u> when, even at meals, he <u>permanently</u> began to wear a hat.

58   The old man lay down in the middle of the road. The cars stopped and people, <u>assuming</u> he was ill, rushed over to <u>establish</u> what was wrong and to offer help and <u>sympathy</u>, but he just grinned and said he was fine. They tried to <u>persuade</u> him to move but he refused. One driver, who was making an <u>urgent</u> <u>delivery</u>, was so <u>furious</u> that his face went <u>scarlet</u> with rage.

Two policemen arrived and told the old man he was causing a <u>serious</u> <u>traffic</u> jam, and he just smiled when they asked him to <u>accompany</u> them to the police station. In the end they lifted him up like a sack and carried him to the pavement. The reason for his strange <u>behaviour</u> remained a <u>mystery</u>. (*125 words*)

59   The class were left alone for a while to finish the <u>preparation</u> for their homework. The <u>prospect</u> of writing for half an hour did not really appeal to Charlie and he decided to <u>indulge</u> in his favourite <u>occupation</u> of <u>imitating</u> anyone in <u>authority</u>, including the teachers.

He walked to the front of the class and <u>immediately</u> <u>launched</u> into his <u>impression</u> of the headmaster. He was very good, so

100

good that his <u>imitation</u> of the headmaster's voice and walk could be easily <u>recognized</u> by anyone who knew him. Charlie's <u>audience</u> laughed and <u>applauded</u> but the clapping suddenly stopped and everyone looked towards the door. No one had <u>realized</u> that the headmaster had been standing there, and had watched all of Charlie's little <u>exhibition</u>. (*122 words*)

60 John was woken by an <u>immense</u> noise and a <u>brilliant</u> light filled his room. He stumbled over to the window and leaned against the <u>radiator</u> while he looked down at the street. A <u>procession</u> of people, many of whom were <u>familiar</u> to him, were <u>skilfully</u> dancing and <u>curving</u> their way up the road, then someone <u>issued</u> an order to stop and everyone stood still while one man peered at his watch.

John waited in <u>suspense</u> and <u>horror</u> to see the outcome of this <u>peculiar</u> <u>ceremony</u>. The silence was softly broken by the chiming of a clock, and on the last and twelfth stroke the dancers all cheered. John was suddenly struck by the <u>knowledge</u> that it was New Years Eve. It was the beginning of a new day and a new year. (*132 words*)